Reimagining Education

edited by Louise Regan and Ian Duckett

First published in 2020 by the Socialist Educational Association
with Manifesto Press
© Socialist Educational Association

ISBN 978-1-907464-46-1
Typset in Bodoni and Gill
Printed in Ireland by Sprint-print

This book is dedicated to Nina Franklin 1952-2020
Nina spent her life fighting for a better education system and for a more peaceful, inclusive world. Our job is to carry on that fight in her footsteps.
Rest in power Nina

Contents

Foreword

Rebecca Long Bailey, *former Shadow Education Secretary*

For those in education, be that children, university students or apprentices, the future may seem unsure at the moment as our whole world is put on pause. But one thing we know for sure is that our education sector and all those who work in it, from teachers to support staff, have risen to the challenge spectacularly. Teaching staff across the country have kept children's education going whilst they are at home and schools have provided a vital service to vulnerable children and the children of key workers.

But as we look forward to life after Covid-19, and the reopening of schools, something that can only happen when it is unequivocally safe to do so, we must recognise that if we are to provide our children with a passport to their future, we cannot return to the status quo.

The inequalities we knew existed between children have been laid bare for all to see. We cannot try to gloss over them. Too many children are living in poverty, many of whom are in working households. Too many families are reliant on free school meals and food banks to keep food on the table each week. And for too many children, their life prospects are determined before they've even started secondary schools.

We cannot simply return to a system that has created these outcomes, now is the time to reform for the better, working with school leaders, teachers and all those who work in schools. After all, they are the frontline and they know what is best for children's and young adults' education.

We can't just applaud the work of schools in supporting the nation's children. A better way to show we appreciate their value is to start giving schools the resources they need after a decade of deep cuts to school budgets and local council support services.

This means addressing structural problems in education which affect children's schooling such as the pressure placed on teachers and their workload, the unsustainably low teacher retention rate, the form of exams and assessments at all school stages and the way achievement at a school level is measured. We must also end the creeping commercialisation of education and return academies to local control.

The Labour Party has said we will replace Ofsted with a new body with responsibility for inspections, designed to drive school improvement and we will scrap the planned new baseline assessment test for children starting school. These are just two examples of the measures needed to reform our education system. This crisis has shown that there is more than one way of providing education, awarding qualifications and measuring success; we must build on that.

We must look again at our education system to ensure that access to a good education is truly a right for every single child, whatever their circumstances and that teaching staff are valued as they should be.

Education is indeed the passport to the future, but it is also one of our most vital tools in rebuilding a more equal society.

Introduction

We started 2020 in the shadow of a general election where the Tory Party increased their majority and we faced a further five years of an austerity government. A government that would pursue further privatisation, continue the test driven school system and would push more of our families and communities in to poverty.

At that time I don't think any of us could have imagined the events that have shaken our world following the outbreak and rapid spread of COVID 19. It is clear that our government has not handled the crisis well. They were slow to react and take any effective measures to stop the spread of COVID and they continue to lack clarity or a clear idea about the management of further outbreaks. The focus seems to be on getting business and the economy going rather than ensuring the health and safety of workers and their families.

Trade union membership and engagement has risen during the pandemic as the unions were at the forefront of pushing the government to take action. The National Education Union has been particularly effective in initially pushing the government to close education settings (just to point out that the majority of education settings stayed open for the children of key workers and vulnerable children and young people), the five tests set by the Union before any wider school opening took place were clear and concise. They were widely shared by politicians, local councils and education workers as a key demand. Leading up to wider school opening the Union launched a ten step recovery plan really focusing on what children, young people and education workers would need.

Many of us have recognised that our education system is broken, it was broken pre COVID. It wasn't broken by educators or children and young people; it was broken by successive government interference. The system has become fragmented and underfunded, our children and young people face an exam factory system with constant testing and a dull, narrow curriculum. Ofsted is not fit for purpose and appears to be there simply to terrorise staff and ensure compliance with government initiatives.

The pause that lockdown created has made many people realise that it is now time for change. We have an opportunity to reclaim our education system and to create a system which truly meets the needs of our children and young people.

This booklet gathers together the thoughts of educators from early years through to higher education. It starts to look at what we have learnt from the crisis and what we need going forward.

The period of lockdown and the recent events following wider opening of society has been extremely challenging for many people – increases in stress, anxiety and trauma for many.

Finally the recent Black Lives Matters protests and the call for our curriculum to be decolonised is an essential part of the work we need to do to reclaim our curriculum and to support children and young people to understand the world that they live in.

"Education is the most powerful weapon which you can use to change the world."
Nelson Mandela

Louise Regan

Re-imagining education and seizing a new initiative: transforming learner engagement and assessment in a changing world
Re-imagining education post COVID19

Zilke Zander

How do we think children can engage in learning/education in that many schools won't open until at least September?

WE KNOW that this won't happen but think the curriculum should have been suspended for the duration of the pandemic on the basis that some pupils (from better off backgrounds) will do all school work set (and more); some won't do any; a lot will do some and of those, they will do different aspects of it. As a result, the gap will be even wider than it was, disadvantage will increase and schools will have to cover everything again anyway. It should have been replaced with an emergency curriculum based on stimulating multi-disciplinary or personal social and health education (PSHE)/citizenship based projects aimed at developing generic learning skills like communication and problem-solving. We know that this won't happen, but it does provide the germ of an idea: what is becoming increasingly known as 'build back better'.

Any student of politics will appreciate the dictum "never let a good crisis go to waste". So let us follow that advice and imagine how education post COVID19 can be improved. Similarly, any progressive educator will see the opportunity to develop the curriculum and assessment strategies in a way more fit for the modern world. Teachers like health care professionals, although not to the same terrible extent, have suffered the neglect of a decade of austerity and now must grasp the current crisis's upending of accepted wisdom to enhance their professional agency, whilst there is understanding of the value of experts. I am referring to exams here, alongside even the *Daily Telegraph* which, on April 21st ran a piece asking if the temporary cancellation should be made permanent. (https://www.telegraph.co.uk/education-and-careers/2020/04/21/exams-cancelled-year-time-scrap-gcses-altogether/). This finally acknowledges an argument education professionals have been advancing for years, that teachers' professional judgments should be recognised as of more value than a snap shot of student performance. Transforming education and re-imagining it should be a priority for progressive educators post-pandemic.

Education after lockdown

The earliest revelation for many in the current crisis, was who the real key workers of society are, and teachers are on this list, although not in the same way as health workers for sound and obvious reasons and this offers another revelation about the place and status of the teaching profession. Teaching has often been referred to as a 'Cinderella' profession where politicians will regularly refer to teachers as professionals akin to doctors in times of demanding something from them, but then when it comes to the practicality of pay, conditions and professional autonomy, are happy to dismiss the views of these same public servants, with disastrous consequences for both teachers and students. Many outside the profession will be familiar with how unattractive it has become through headlines of the numbers who have left it due to disgust with Govian reforms, unlimited workload and accompanying stress. These factors underpin the most demoralising issue: the lack of professional status. As teachers ourselves, now of too many years to count and eight years respectively, we have survived the first milestone of five years service, after which a reported 30 – 40 per cent quit and are now contemplating leaving the profession before the ten year milestone which is frequently reported as a point by which 50 per cent leave. The conflict between what teaching should be and what it is, are the reasons why I am excited – for the first time in a long time – by the potential for a brave new world of education.

Back to exams. If they can be forgone this summer and students still progress into employment, apprenticeships or university as it is expected to the point of certainty that they will, then why return to them? The case for exams is as follows: They are dispassionate and anonymous; they are standardised thus fair; they allow for results that are easily understood; they enable schools and teachers to be held to account by providing a way of measuring school achievement in terms of how many students achieve 'good' results. This final point is the critical one as it is the most significant reason why many politicians are loathe to replace exams. It is also why ending exams as we know it would be such a radical transformation, as it would shift the balance of power in favour of classroom professionals in a way politicians are unwilling to do, as it would create a self-confident profession possessing autonomy on an inconvenient scale.

A fresh approach to assessment

In terms of the other arguments in favour of exams they are not strong and I am not proposing a system of no examination or assessment as there is of course still a role for exams – ones created, administered, assessed and then peer-reviewed by serving teachers. To those unfamiliar with how current 'standardised' GCSEs and A Levels work, they are hardly fair or effective systems. The evidence of the stress caused by them is legion. British students are the most over tested in Europe and rates of poor mental health and even suicide are rising steadily, linked to exam overload at the end of two years of 'crammed' study. The whole experience of too many students in too many schools is blighted by an exam factory mentality where all efforts throughout schooling are geared towards passing a test rather than any more humane or enriching purpose. It is a cruel irony given how the ease of understanding an exam score is often cited as a benefit of the system, that very few outside education fully understand the 'standardisation' process that goes into our standardised exams. From my experience of trying to explain this to both parents and students when they ask the common question of what grade I predict come exam time, the sheer unfairness and also inexpert nature of the process comes through. Most people assume simple quantities pass marks for exams exist and if a student surpasses a certain number of marks they get a corresponding grade. They don't. The point at which grades are allocated is worked out through a bizarre statistical process predicated on the logic that certain numbers of children will achieve certain grades and then working out what actual exam marks equate to grades, so as to enable the specified number of children to achieve them or not – as the case is for many children who fall on the wrong side of the grading tracks. The only commonly understood element of this is that grade boundaries shift in relation to how well a cohort performs – if there is strong performance across the board – up the grade boundaries go and vice versa. There is much more that can be said of this system but for our purpose here, it is clearly not simple and more importantly, it is clearly no more 'scientific' than the judgment of a skilled educator.

Then there is the logistical process of creating and then assessing these exams through a bureaucratic labyrinth comprising multiple "competing" exam boards which are mostly "edu businesses", some charities, and a host of quangos. Regardless of exact status, all take public money for people with little or no teaching experience to write vast amounts of literature to tell teachers how to do their jobs. Schools must then spend more of their portion of the nation's education budget on buying supporting materials such as text books from these bodies. Here it is important to note the presence of edu-businesses, most significantly Pearson, which is the education world's answer to the likes of Capita and G4S taking public funds, in the name of outsourced efficiency, but in reality providing distanced service devoid of true attachment to its purpose.

Many teachers then mark exam papers for these cartels in a manner prescribed, it would seem, entirely to remove professional judgment. This is not a scientific study of the economics, but the costs of compensating teachers through higher salaries to take on some of these roles independently, would undoubtedly be less than the sums spent on this outsourcing of professional agency. For starters any pay rises would be minimal as all teachers would prize the increased professional autonomy and status derived from being the true gate keepers of educational standards, above any change to their contracts measured in pounds and pence. But the gains would be more long term and although less friendly to the eyes of accountants, no more significant for the health of the education sector. Nye Bevan the founder of the NHS frequently defended the cost of the health service by pointing to a ledger overlooked on the balance sheet, that of the cost saved to the country and the revenues generated by all those quickly treated by the NHS and returned swiftly to active life. The same parallel should be drawn with education. The sums lost through stress-related sick leave by teachers who are not masters of their own fates are vast. As is the waste of human capital and training expenditure on all those who leave the profession after a few years or those who never even enter a classroom having had their fill on a training year. This is not to mention how much harder it is for teachers to do their jobs faced with stressed out students who again teachers are largely disempowered to truly help, due to the lack of control over the assessments at the root of the stress. If teachers were to seize the means of educational production so to speak, think of the possibilities for progress in all these areas it would create. It will be a long process but the work of the SEA and unions should be to advance these ideas now, whilst there is the intellectual space to think so radically and whilst we are faced with a Labour party in need of policies which can present it as a government in waiting with answers it wants to implement not just things it wants to criticise.

On the cusp of education and social care

So, what can we do to seize the initiative post-pandemic? We can apply some of the progressive emergency curriculum and radical learning strategies used in the time of crisis.

In a world where teachers stand at the cusp of education and social care, learner engagement is a complex business. As with the urgent need to find more fitting assessment models in mainstream education, the current pandemic has thrown engagement into even sharper focus. It is concerned not only with straightforward engagement, but with learning and developing skills of employability and enterprise and is increasingly directed at those on re-engagement and intervention programmes in schools, colleges, alternative provision and home education schemes.

New ways of engaging

Learner engagement should determine a curriculum that is meaningful and personalised and one which will foster the development of personal learning, thinking and employability skills in a safe environment for all 14+ learners.

This curriculum outline is based on an entitlement model and is, at the same time, developmental and aspirational. With English and Maths at its heart and with engagement, enterprise and employability as its chief objectives, the curriculum will emphasise personal and social development and provide vocational tasters. Learning is supported by regular 1:1 coaching sessions and target-setting reviews; Personal, Social, Health Education (PSHE) and citizenship and a wide-range of enrichment activities aimed at enhancing the overall learning experience.

Engagement activities

There are three main curriculum components to any engagement programme that are meaningful and of the real world. These are leadership, employability and volunteering. It is also designed to deliver the following attributes to all participants:
- Team-work
- Target setting and skills for learning
- Problem solving
- Language and Communication

An engagement or re-engagement programme should be assignment-based and focus on the learner; rather than on set, weekly sessions. It should be a tailored learning resource, based on agreed, realistic targets that take account of the needs of each individual learner.

Engagement and re-engagement activities might include:

1 Introductory Skills session – what will you need to succeed? Team-work; target setting and skills for learning; problem solving; language and communication.

2 Describe Yourself – using a method of your choice (written description, picture, film or artefact), try to explain who you are. You should think about your background, ambitions and words which describe you. Record your evidence.

3 Objects that represent your life – bring in three objects which represent who you are. Discuss with a partner or in a group what they represent and why you have brought them.

4 Research a topic that interests you – use the internet, library, newspaper or another route to find out information about a subject of your choice. Present the information in an interesting or original way.

5 Discuss career options with other people in your group. Which areas of work would you like to follow and what qualifications or skills do you need to get there?

6 Things I'm good at/could do better – make a list of things which you are already good at. This can be academic subjects but should also include other skills which you have. Then list things which you would like to improve in the short and long-term. Keep a record of your thoughts.

As well as developing skills to enable teachers to support learners on their personalised learning programmes, learner engagement sets out to equip learners with Personal, Learning and Thinking Skills (PLTS) who are:

- Independent enquirers
- Creative thinkers
- Reflective learners
- Team workers
- Self-managers
- Effective participators

Many will dismiss these proposals as utopian – dismissing the professionalism of teachers – which is understandable given that the government makes no effort to present teachers as expert professionals. What the current crisis proves however is that teachers are key workers. You can take away the exams and associated bureaucracy as has been done and teachers still innovate in delivering learning opportunities for students who will still progress to the next stage of their lives. Take the teachers out of this and the exam boards cannot fill their roles. Is it really utopian to suggest teachers be free to exercise the full professional agency their status deserves? After all teachers' working conditions are children's learning conditions and if this crisis can create a better understanding of how to enhance these then it will not have been wasted. At the end of it all, post-coronavirus, re-imagining education and seizing a new initiative, as well as protecting these gains, should be a rallying call for radical educators.

Ian Duckett and Chris Smith

A radical vision for Early Childhood Care and Education [1]

Introduction

THE EARLY YEARS (which we define as the period immediately following the end of parental leave to compulsory school age) is in many ways the 'Cinderella' of phases within the English education system. Though many see this phase as one of the most important in a child's education, this sector suffers from low status, confused provision, inadequate funding and a generally poor level of qualifications within its workforce. We feel it is time to challenge this status quo – the Early Years deserve a greater prominence in political thinking about education provision generally, and within Labour's vision of a National Education Service (NES).

Calder and Rea (2019) discussed terminology in the context of the 2006 Childcare Act which they argue, falsely divided child 'care' from the 'education' of children. Instead, they put forward the term 'Early Childhood Care and Education'. This terminology is adopted throughout in what follows.

Whenever 'education' is introduced into Early Years discourse, some will think automatically of schools and schooling. This need not be the case. We believe passionately in age/stage-appropriate, play-based learning for children. We do not discuss curriculum in this short paper as we feel the current Early Years curriculum to be largely uncontentious, save for the increasing pressure on it to make children 'school ready' by a focus on narrowing outcome measures. We would argue that the opposite is needed. That is, that play based pedagogy should spread further and more widely into primary schools rather than schooling pushing onto Early Childhood Care and Education provision.

What characterises good Early Childhood Care and Education?

Our holistic vision of Early Childhood Care and Education envisages a safe but rich environment accessible by all, where young children are cared for and can thrive and where parents can confidently leave their children, knowing that their physical, emotional and intellectual needs will be met by a well-qualified and expert workforce.

A good example of holistic care and education is Sure Start introduced in 1998 by a Labour government. It is a credit to Labour – and not least to Angela Rayner (Shadow Secretary of State for Education 2016-2020) – that the renewal of Sure Start is a promise. Sure Start Children's Centres are places where families with young children can access facilities and receive the support that they need. In practice, they are for expectant parents and those with a child up to 5 years old. This includes any or all of the following:

● Pre/Ante and Post-natal care/classes
● Parenting classes
● Breast-feeding support

- Nursery care and education
- Toddler groups with professional support in attendance
- Speech therapy
- Back to work advice for parents

In addition, they are places where professional staff are able to pick up early indications of special educational needs, domestic abuse and child neglect, thus enabling early interventions.

Since the 2010 general election, Sure Start has been run down as a result of austerity measures. There is a desperate need for it to be fully re-instated and extended.

What does the post Covid landscape look like?

As stated above, the current Early Years curriculum is largely uncontentious and may be considered 'fit for purpose'.

Early Childhood Care and Education provision is surprisingly diverse. The type of provision includes:
- Childminders
- Day nurseries
- Nursery schools
- Pre-reception classes in schools

The landscape is further complicated by the mixed economy of providers. Early Childhood Care and Education may be provided by private individuals, limited companies, the voluntary sector, independent schools (the so-called PVI – private voluntary and independent) as well as local authorities.

Standing over this diverse provision within its mixed economy there are elements of public involvement. Local Authorities administer central government funding and have a responsibility to ensure there are sufficient places to cater for local needs. The sector is inspected by Ofsted.

In the late 1980s funding for childcare was made available for all four-year-olds and some three year-old children. Labour's 2006 Childcare Act extended this provision, and 15 hours of free childcare was offered for all children aged three. Once the benefits of this provision for children were realised, the offer was extended, and 15 hours was also offered to the two year-old children from poorer families. This was often in families where the parents were not working, with a clear emphasis on education and children's rights. The 2010 coalition government extended the offer of free childcare to 30 hours for working families with three and four year-old children (emphasis on child care again). Whilst the children who would most likely benefit the most from more time in nursery, the three year-olds from poorer families, are confined to the statutory 15 hours.

Calder and Rea (2019) believe that many vulnerable children are missing out on appropriate Early Years education because the current government is trapped within a 'care' discourse.

Within this mixed economy, over 84 per cent of provision for children aged three and under three is being run by for-profit concerns, while 60 per cent of provision for children aged between three and five is being run by for-profit operators, (though many small, private sector nurseries rely almost exclusively on the Government 15/30 hours funding and, because the level of this funding is low, are not making profit. Some have recently closed because of this). The complex and confusing way in which the 15/30 hours offers need to be claimed rather than directly funding the Early Years settings, has increased inequalities in a myriad of ways: for example, the requirement for parents to re-confirm eligibility for 30 hours' entitlement every three months, where parents may be self-employed and/or working in the 'gig economy'.

There is a reliance on outsourced providers and an increasingly fragmented system, which we see as undesirable. This will pose a challenge for Labour in office. We suggest the Party starts now to plan how a comprehensive state provision of Early Childhood Care and Education will sit within the NES.

The Early Childhood Care and Education workforce: qualifications, pay and gender

Partly because it is poorly funded, partly because some high-end private operators cream off profits and partly because of the effect of the 'care' discourse on pay and conditions, the Early Years sector is characterised by a heavily female gendered, largely poorly qualified [2] and low paid workforce.

For example, the starting salary for a newly qualified primary school teacher educated to degree level is £23,720, whilst the average rate of pay for an experienced Early Years teacher – also qualified to degree level – is around £15,000. She, and it will in all likely hood be she, will receive only statutory minimum holidays and statutory sick pay. Career progression is minimal.

The sector is largely non-unionised. However, we see an opportunity for the National Education Union to embrace Early Years professionals as members which we believe will help to 'level up the pay and conditions of the early childhood workforce.

The Early Years workforce development in England study (Bonetti, 2020)[3], examined key Early Years policies implemented since 2006 and focussed on how governments can provide the right incentives for the sector to employ and retain highly qualified and skilled practitioners. The sector has lived through a decade of frequent policy changes, many of which were short-lived, disconnected and implemented without extra resources to support the sector.

The Graduate Leader Fund (GLF) [established in 2007] provided PVIs with financial incentives to recruit graduates. The GLF was successful in setting the sector on a path towards increasing workers' qualification levels. Between 2007 and 2011, when ring-fenced funding totaled £305 million, the number of workers holding a first degree or a foundation degree increased by 76 per cent, from 16,500 workers to 29,100 workers, and the number of workers holding a higher degree or other degree increased by 13 per cent, from 5,200 workers to 5,900 workers. The proportion of degree qualified professionals increased by approximately five percentage points, from seven per cent of PVIs staff in

2007 to 12 per cent in 2011. Settings which gained a graduate leader under these initiatives made significant improvements in quality for pre-school children (DFE 2011).

We argue that a graduate professional workforce for Early Childhood Care and Education ought to be a long-term aspiration for a Labour government. In the short and medium term, a profession led by appropriately qualified graduates with well-trained support (following the model of teachers and teaching assistants in other educational settings) is attainable. There is plenty of opportunity to access appropriate courses in England, but more needs to be done to achieve effective integration of such courses with any requirement for workers to have such a degree, for the supervision of practice to be properly funded, and as mentioned earlier, for qualifications to be linked with appropriate pay and career prospects. This may be at the outset of a career or in-service and could use the most up-to-date examples of place-based and blended professional learning opportunities.

It is widely accepted that less than two per cent of the Early Childhood Care and Education workforce is male [4]. In the longer term, more should be done to address the gender imbalance in Early Years as positive male role models are important to young children, some of whom do not have these at home.

What is school readiness?

Much has been thought, said and written about children's readiness for school[5], far less about the readiness for schools to receive young children. Perhaps the Covid-19 hiatus provides the opportunity to redress this balance.

UNICEF considers three elements to school readiness:

● Children's readiness for school (which is related to their learning and development, such as communication skills, personal, social and emotional and physical development)

● Families' readiness for school (which concerns attachment and home/school liaison), and

● Schools' readiness for children (ensuring learning environments are child-friendly and adapt to the diverse needs of young learners and their families)

Here, we are focusing on the latter – the readiness for schools to receive young children, which can be viewed through the macro (the education system) and/or the micro (individual school) prism. This short paper considers it at only the macro level.

If society were to take seriously the concept of school readiness in terms of the child – call it a child centered approach to school readiness – then it makes sense for children to start school at different times according to when they are ready. In England and Wales a child must start full-time education once they reach compulsory school age. This is the 31 December, 31 March or 31 August following their fifth birthday – whichever comes first. Clearly, there is room here for compromise between the exact point at which an individual child is ready to start school and the three points of entry (September, January and April) each year.

In practice however, most children start school full-time in the September after they turn four. We are mindful that this means many children are starting school too soon, some aged four years and a few days, whereas they need not be in school until they are over five.

The DFE says "if you do not think your child is ready to start school by then, they can start part-way through the year or part time – as long as they are in full-time education by the time they reach 'compulsory school age" [6] but the onus here is very much on the parent to argue for an exception to the norm.

Given the prominence of 'school readiness' within in Early Years discourses it seems to us incongruent that most children start school full-time at a single point – in the September after they turn four. We suggest this practice is a product of the neo-liberalisation of education and comes from a complex web of factors including funding, over-prescriptive curriculum/assessment constraints and league tables.

● For as long as funding follows the child, settings will – understandably – want children on their lists as soon as possible.

● For as long as schools and teachers are judged upon SATs and other test scores, they will want the children in school as soon as possible.

● For as long as the curriculum is prescriptive, teachers will tend to want children to move through it in whole groups and not have new children starting later in the year.

These organisational pressures may not be in the best interest of individual children.

Given that some children are starting school too soon, it seems to us doubly problematic that in many cases children are assessed by teachers in the September or October when they have just started school – following a long summer holiday. There is anecdotal evidence that some school teachers do not trust assessments made by their colleagues practicing in Early Childhood Care and Education settings.

Conclusion

In this short paper we have argued for:

● Removing any compulsion for Early Years discourses to be framed in terms only of 'care' and ensuring we have a more holistic understanding of and approach to, Early Childhood Care and Education.

● That Labour in opposition, plan for a comprehensive offer of age/stage appropriate Early Childhood Care and Education, which includes the extension of Sure Start – available to all from the point where parental leave ends.

● Play-based education – that is good for children, good for families, good for society – to permeate through Early Childhood Care and Education and into infant/primary schools.

● The introduction of a graduate led Early Childhood Care and Education profession in the medium term, working towards a fully graduate profession as a long-term aspiration, with these professionals being appropriately rewarded.

● Adequate funding for all of the above.

● Greater collaboration and professional trust between Early Years and school based professionals.

● Local Authorities, academy trusts and schools should recognise the legal start of compulsory education (the 31 December, 31 March or 31 August following a child's fifth birthday – whichever comes first) and aim to be more child centric and respectful of the needs of individual children.

It is unlikely that Labour will be in office before 2024. This provides time for considered thinking, planning and preparation. This needs to be done now whilst in opposition, so that as soon as Labour is in office it can introduce the NES including Early Childhood Care and Education provision that our children badly need. In the long term – perhaps a second term promise – the nation needs a framework of state built and funded comprehensive nursery provision, non-compulsory, but free at the point of use.

Jane Rea and Tony Rea

Notes

1   This short paper draws from and builds upon Calder P & Rea T What should the NES say about the early years? *Education Politics* No. 137, March 2019 pp. 8-11 and is further informed by a SEA meeting in Bristol held on Saturday 22 February 2020 when we and Arron Bradbury (Nottingham Trent University) presented on early years issues.
2   This is a generalisation and there are exceptions. For example, Jane Rea owns, manages and works hands-on in a small nursery in a deprived south Devon town. She has a BSc, MA, PGCE and EYQTS.
3   https://www.nuffieldfoundation.org/project/analysis-of-the-early-years-workforce-and-its-impact-on-childrens-outcomes
4   Pete Moorhouse https://irresistible-learning.co.uk/resource/men-early-years-thoughts/
5   A search for 'school readiness' using Google Scholar on 29/05/2020 came up with 1,730,000 results.
6   https://www.gov.uk/schools-admissions/school-starting-age

The power lies in our hands – let's teach the children what they need to learn.
Let's give schools back to the children

PEDAGOGY IS the science of teaching and to become a great scientist or indeed a great teacher we must test out our theories because science and teaching is an "empirical" field, that is, it develops a body of knowledge by observing things and it relies on the kind of knowledge that comes from experience. The discussions we have throughout the school day with our colleagues as we reflect on what we are doing and how to make it better is what makes us the practical and reflective experts that know how our children are learning, because after all that is why we are there, to enable children to learn.

This is because as teachers we recognise that we are the facilitators for what is most important and that is the learning. The science of teaching is that we get the outcome of achieving great learners. Children who are able to ask questions and respond to their surroundings with empathy, a desire to challenge what is unjust and search for new solutions.

In our primary classrooms currently, we are working to a system that has teachers who are battling with this regime every day. The reason is because of what is driving the primary school agenda and therefore the curriculum and sadly the way it is delivered.

The power base has been removed from the schools because everything is being externally driven through Ofsted, performance related pay and standardised testing. Primary children are now tested or assessed for national data five times during their primary education – that is every other year. This, of course, does not include the countless assessment weeks, practice tests, and the good old-fashioned spellings and times tables tests that they face week in week out.

We are creating an environment in which we are conditioning our children to fear failure who know that they are being measured and that if they fall short of the standard expected of them, they will need to do more of the same and probably fail again.

Children are told they have failed to reach an expected standard because they have not ticked off a predetermined set of skills. But who is it that has set these skills? Who is it that is deciding that a child has failed in learning in their primary education and should be labelled in that way? For example, it is clearly important that children should be able read fluently and with understanding and we know that reading is the key to success across all of the learning that we do. So, what are the best indicators of success for lifelong learning for our children? Is it the drilling of speed reading and the tricks to answering the comprehension questions set in those standardised tests? Or maybe it is these three questions designed by fifth graders, in a class taught by Rafe Esquith who wrote the book 'Teach like you hair is on fire'. These children believe they are a much more accurate test of their reading proficiency:

"**1.** Have you ever secretly read under your desk in school because the teacher was boring and you were dying to finish the book you were reading?

2. Have you ever been scolded for reading at the dinner table?

3. Have you ever read secretly under the covers after beeing told to go to bed?"[1]

Compare this to the findings of the research carried out by the National Union of Teachers in 2015 that led to The Exam Factories Report that stated:

"One aim of accountability measures is to improve attainment. There is evidence that high stakes testing results in an improvement in test scores because teachers focus their teaching very closely on the test. Test scores do not necessarily represent pupils' overall level of understanding and knowledge, but rather, the fact that teachers are focusing their teaching very strongly on preparing pupils for the test." [2]

The purpose of what we are doing has become blurred. We are not looking far enough into the future and whilst pedagogy is a science there is also an art in how we create the conditions in which the children can learn and continue to learn. It is not our job to provide the State with data through short term learning that can be measured and judged, it is our job to enable learning. That is the skill we must teach. It is a more difficult skill and it requires considerable art and science combined. It requires teachers to react to changing circumstances and to individual children. This is something that takes time to learn as a teacher and something that teachers never stop learning.

As teachers what we learn about teaching is vitally important in shaping the way we work with the children we teach. Having the opportunity to explore the impact of a particular strategy or method that we have been developing and peer reviewing is fundamental to developing practise. Action research into teaching is part of our science. Unfortunately, the reality of the CPD (continuing professional development) that takes place is that a new external initiative is introduced, developed with children from a different community than the one in which we teach. They will more than likely have a different learning profile than the children you will be working with, and you are instructed to implement it and then you are evaluated to see how well it has been implemented against a set of targets matched to a set of data goals.

Where have the children gone?

What happened to recognising the child who recently arrived in the country?

What happened to the child who is dealing with extreme poverty and comes into school every day, but is hungry and exhausted?

What happened to the child who is suffering from anxiety and the fact that they are in school at all is a huge achievement?

This of course is not only an issue for primary schools in the UK but it is a global phenomenon. The Chicago Teachers Union have researched and published their findings in *The Schools Chicago's Students Deserve* [3]. They outline in the *Pedagogy of Poverty*, how standardised testing is used as a tool to segregate educational opportunities and how the system it creates compounds discrimination. Together with inequalities in housing, employment, education, and health care and shows how all these factors contribute to the achievement gap. The research also recognises that the emphasis has increasingly been on test scores and other student data, despite putting on the façade of providing the need for what we refer to as a broad and balanced curriculum. They also recognise that in most schools, particularly those that are struggling or have been negatively 'labelled' or 'categorised' any CPD or staff meetings are dominated by looking at data, analysing data, and talking about how to "improve (data) outcomes,"[3] when it should also be a time for professional collaboration and/ or learning.

This poverty of pedagogy is further exacerbated by teacher evaluation systems that exist globally and that include the performance related pay of teachers that was introduced in 2014 in England. These systems rely on test data to determine teacher 'effectiveness'. What is becoming ever increasingly apparent is that what is missing is a system that supports the development of pedagogy that is culturally relevant to the children and that is delivered to the children in a way that they can continue to enjoy learning rather than to fear failing.

Margaret Donaldson wrote in the opening paragraph of her book 'Children's Minds',
"When we make laws which compel our children to go to school we assume collectively an awesome responsibility. For a period of ten years, with minor variations from country to country the children are conscripts; and their youth does nothing to alter the seriousness of the fact. Nor is it altered by the intention, however genuine, that the school experience should be 'for their good'."[4]

We therefore have a responsibility to make their experience a good experience. To ensure that those eager, lively, happy children who enter our primary schools full of spontaneity ready to explore, discover and create do not leave those same schools feeling defeated with a bitter taste. At the same time we must create the conditions in which these children can develop the skills they need to read and write, to become numerate and of course to rejoice in creativity.

The exam factories system we are creating in our schools has been described as 'deeply damaging' for our children. It is a system that not only builds fear of failure into learning as has been outlined but it also works towards an end product of individual achievement and competition. It does not encourage collaboration and team work, which must be the best way to solve a problem and overcome a challenge. Our classrooms are generating a group of disaffected children and this comes on top of the fact that, after government intervention, the curriculum does not reflect the children's lives but is becoming increasingly knowledge based. That knowledge is narrowing and culturally biased and does not reflect the achievements of women and girls. **There is no place for them to be active learners but instead children's role is to passively accept and internalise what they are told rather than learn to think for themselves. And, of course, teachers and support staff in their children's schools have not had any say in what is 'the best' or 'core' for the children to be internalising and regurgitating.**

Teachers are under enormous pressure to meet targets and prove that they are able to close attainment gaps and this means they feel forced to comply with the delivery of a curriculum that is about coverage and targets and ticking boxes rather than responding to the individuality of the children they are currently teaching. This does not mean you waste time or take away the pace of learning, it means you don't waste time covering a scheduled learning outcome the majority of your class is not ready to learn. Children live in fear of stepping out of line in classrooms to say they don't understand, to ask a question at the 'wrong' time, to ask for a little longer to complete a story that they are thoroughly enjoying writing. Or to question why they are learning about something. Or to state they find something boring. Or to explain why they lost their temper. Time is a very precious commodity in primary schools and restorative justice takes more time than 'Don't do that again!' Yet in the long run its value and educational worth is immeasurable.

In a restorative school more emphasis is put on personal responsibility of the children. When conflict happens, there is a structure to resolve it. It allows children, and indeed educators, to learn from their mistakes so mistakes aren't repeated over and over. Again, it requires training and investment, whether it be time or funding, but surely it is worth it. When children were asked to talk about the benefits of restorative justice for the Restorative Justice Council they said, "Even if you are young you can intervene in problems and make sure everything's all right."[5] They also acknowledged that they needed training. This recurrent theme of training whether it is for children or the adults in school highlights the need for investing in them and the teachers and support staff who work in our schools. This training must be about enabling children to learn rather than forcing teachers and support staff to follow doctrines.

The biproduct of these fulfilled children will of course be fulfilled teachers. And probably the biproduct of fulfilled teachers is happy children who will be more effective learners.

At this turbulent time when primary schools have been faced with operating in a completely different way and national tests have been cancelled, we have the opportunity to take a breath and re-evaluate, to reclaim the good practice and re-establish what is important. To collectively take responsibility.

We should start with the basic principles that our schools should be places where all our children feel safe, secure and welcome. If you visit schools' websites you will discover ethos statements that say that everyone will be respected, irrespective of race, religion or gender in addition to this everyone will be valued and their individuality will be respected and the children will be offered a broad and balanced curriculum. In reality we know that schools are working hard to overcome very difficult societal inequalities and discriminatory behaviour and so whilst this may be their aim there is still a long way to go and it is important to acknowledge this. In recent research by the National Education Union and UK Feminsta the report *It's Just Everywhere* states

> *"Over a third (34%) of primary school teachers say they witness gender stereotyping in their school on at least a weekly basis. Over half (54%) say they witness it on at least a termly basis."* [6] *Sexism is endemic in our schools and without the curriculum*

and space to unpick the established layers of sexism and stereotyping that exist it will remain in place.

With the global response to the murder of George Floyd at the hands of the police in Minneapolis on 25 May 2020, children in all our schools will once again be party to the debate around racism. Therefore, teachers must be responsible for enabling them to talk about how this makes them feel and how they think society should respond. Children and teachers need the skills to manage these discussions and to explore the history that has led us to where we are today. They need to have the doors to that history opened to them. We cannot hide from the past. Once again this leads us to question whether CPD opportunities have enabled teachers to provide a school experience that is any good. Are we able to access CPD to make a significant cultural change in our schools?

We cannot lay responsibility for the changes required with individual teachers. We must have a collective response to the changes we need to make. These changes are long overdue. We have missed many opportunities. Following the McPherson Report some Local Authorities responded with action plans but the changes have not had the necessary impact and they have not been embedded.

This year the Standardised assessments were cancelled. The children will not suffer as a result. Children are going to need to be supported on their return to school. They are going to need to be reintroduced into school and helped back into learning through a programme of PSHE. Many children will be returning and feeling anxious and a significant number of children will have been through trauma during the period when they have been out of school. For teachers to do the best and to take on this 'awesome responsibility' they are going to need to be given the training and the trust to do just that. As scientists in the art of education they can already tell you that the very last thing they need is a narrow curriculum that constrains them and does not allow for group work and collaboration. We need to let our children explore and take control of their own learning knowing that they can make mistakes and everything will be all right because school is somewhere you come to learn and learning is fun.

Philipa Harvey

Notes

1   *Teach Like Your Hair is On Fire The methods and madness inside Room 56* – Rafe Esquith 2007
2   *Exam Factories. The impact of accountability on children and young people*. – Research commissioned by the National Union of Teachers – Marryn Hutchins
3   *The Schools Chicago Student's Deserve – Research-based Proposals To Strengthen Elementary And Secondary Education In The Chicago Public Schools*. Issued by the Chicago Teachers Union Primary research support from Carol R. Caref, Ph.D., Coordinator, CTU Quest Center Pavlyn C. Jankov, Researcher, CTU Quest Center.2012
4   *Children's Minds*- Margaret Donaldson 1978
5   https://restorativejustice.org.uk/resources/restorative-practice-schools
6   https://neu.org.uk/advice/its-just-everywhere-sexism-schools#sexist-language

The world has changed – let's change the world

SINCE THE closure of schools on 20 March 2020, staff working in education have been doing our best to adjust to a new reality and trying to respond to the crisis that has engulfed us all. We have had to make huge adjustments to life and learning in a pandemic. Huge efforts are being made across the country to meet the needs of students and families and to support staff who are trying to work in entirely unprecedented circumstances.

It has been a steep learning curve and has made those of us working in education reflect on some key questions:
- What is learning for?
- How can we meet the needs of our young people?
- What are those needs – and how have they changed?

Of course, many of us have been questioning the trajectory of the English education system for years, conscious that it follows the demands of governmental ideology not the needs of children. We have been operating in a neo-liberal exam-factory model of education which has led to our young people apparently being among the most tested – and discontented – children in the world. It is too often a model in which children are inculcated with knowledge rather than one in which they are partners. Exploration, creativity, investigation all take a back seat.

And it is a system which has had its funding stripped for a decade with the poorest schools and the poorest children facing the hardest cuts. It is a system of setting and streaming and testing and failing. It is a system in which the curriculum too often reflects the whims of individuals at the DFE rather than the real experience, heritage, interest or needs of the young people it is imposed on, or indeed years of research and experience from experts in the field.

At secondary level in England, it is a system that has seen a narrowing of the curriculum as space on the timetable for the arts, sport and Modern Foreign Languages has been squeezed resulting in fewer students taking arts subjects at GCSE & A Level and the lowest level of MFL teaching in the UK. It has also failed to close the attainment gap for disadvantaged pupils. If you are poor, Black, have special educational needs or all three, then the system is failing you more than it fails everyone else.

The figures on exclusions show our current system disproportionately fails our Black students, young people with special needs and those who are living in poverty. A grassroots movement, including groups like No More Exclusions, is gaining momentum but this is an issue which needs addressing by government to ensure lasting change.

Our education system is not a success by any stretch of the imagination. It is sobering to think that its chief architects, Michael Gove and Dominic Cummings, remain at the heart of government and are leading figures in the response to the Covid-19 pandemic. Their reckless unwillingness to heed experts which has caused so much damage in education is now creating havoc with people's lives.

But in some ways, this pandemic has actually allowed staff to insist on putting children's needs first for once. In the short term, it has meant a complete readjustment to trying to teach and learn at a distance and it has allowed us to test the hypothesis that technology is the answer to all our woes.

Many of our young people still do not have access to the internet or even to computers. A survey by Education Institute of Scotland showed that 60% of teachers said students did not have access to suitable technology to access learning from home. There will be variations in these figures but there are plenty of regions across the UK where internet access is unreliable and the high rates of poverty mean that access to suitable technology will be patchy. Anecdotally, it is clear that large numbers of young people are simply not accessing on-line learning and schools and colleges are sending out paper packs of work in the post. There are clearly some benefits to the inclusion of on-line learning in our educational toolkit but we will have to address this inequality of provision first.

However, even when our students are accessing the resources, many of them are struggling to make sense of the work in isolation and without a teacher or teaching assistant to support them. Differentiating work on-line is hard to do and highlights the myriad ways that education staff intervene in thousands of one-to-one interactions face-to-face every day.

Many of our young people will be finding it hard to motivate themselves in a domestic environment which may be overcrowded or in which they have other responsibilities such as helping family with childcare or other chores. Even where young people have technology in the home, they may need to share it with other siblings or family members. And finding a quiet room away from others where they can focus will be a big ask.

It turns out there is more to learning than Google classrooms – even for those that can access it.

It turns out there is more to teaching than a power point presentation and some worksheets.

And it turns out that education is more than teaching to the test.

The fact is that, despite our best efforts, we are not meeting the needs of our young people in this crisis. But it also raises the question, were we doing that even when we were in school?

This pandemic has made us rethink our world and consider if what we are teaching our young people is really what they need to survive and thrive.

What is education for if it cannot meet the needs of our young people?

What is education for if it cannot provide them with the skills they need for a rapidly changing world?

It turns out there is more to teaching and learning after all.

What if, instead of trying to reconfigure a curriculum that is not fit for purpose, we actually went back to the drawing board and created a curriculum that valued all our young people for who they are and where they come from; a curriculum which valued the heritage and history of all our communities; a curriculum which valued our students as citizens of our society and created enough space for them to grow.

Education professionals all over the country have been trying to provide the kind of learning that our children need and, in some places, practices are developing that we should aim to keep and spread when we go back. Staff in many schools are using on-line facilities for cross-subject, collaborative planning and creating imaginative tasks that students can complete at home without need of a computer or access to expensive resources. As well as bringing professionals with different expertise together, staff have been free to think about the needs of the child and the context in which they are learning, making education meaningful and purposeful.

Isn't that what education should be like all the time?

So, what should happen when we go back?

Many people in education are saying that we cannot simply slot back into the way things were but there will be a pressure to return to 'normal'. So, we will have to be proactive in our response and work collectively to propose alternative models of teaching and learning.

Covid-19 is likely to be part of our lives for the foreseeable future and the impact on schools and on staffing will be huge. It simply won't be possible to return to the way things were.

We will need to completely rework the ways in which we teach and support our children's learning. Increasing numbers of young people may return to school or college but a significant number may not. Schools and colleges will need to not only rework the way we teach face-to-face, but also think about how best to provide distance learning and emotional support for those young people who remain at home. Any on-line provision will require significant investment and training for staff.

But, slotting back into the way things are is just not justifiable either. Put simply, we have an obligation to put the needs of our young people first. And those needs will be many. Some will be the same as before but some needs will be very different. Many of those needs will be emotional or social which a testing regime won't address.

So Covid-19 has presented us with a huge set of problems, and it has also exposed the problems that were there before. It also provides us with an opportunity to change the way we do things and build schools and colleges fit for our young people and the world in which they find themselves.

We can ensure that the impact is transformative – in ways that will improve our curriculum.

In the short term we need some kind of recovery curriculum that addresses the emotional needs of our young people. There will be trauma, there will be adjustment from social isolation and behaviour will reflect this.

Rigid, authoritarian regimes will not meet the needs of our young people.

We will need a flexible, responsive curriculum with strong PSHE and pastoral strands. Doing this will be hard with social distancing but it must be done.

The curriculum will need to be adjusted to address the upheaval likely in GCSE and A Level courses as well as the knock-on effect on university, apprenticeships, training and careers. But in the long term, we should interrogate the manner in which we measure achievement and attainment and consider whether the external exams system is driving too much of what we do in education. Workplace practitioners need to be leading this debate especially as the impetus from the DfE will be to keep things as they are.

The issue of testing in primary schools is much clearer. Get rid of it.

It does not meet the needs of the children. In fact, it prevents schools delivering the curriculum children need. It positively inhibits the kind of creative, explorative, investigative learning we should be providing. And it has a detrimental effect on children's mental health.

SATS have been scrapped this year and assessment will be based on formative teacher assessment which begs the question: if we didn't need them this year, why do we need them at all?

This year, even more than other years, there can be no reason to impose Baseline, SATs and all the rigid summative testing. This is not what our young people need.

We should look very hard at the structure of the whole curriculum from nursery, primary through to secondary, sixth form and FE. Before Covid-19, the cracks were there for all to see – a move away from child-centred education; a narrowing of subjects; high levels of stress and anxiety; high rates of exclusion with particular groups (Black, SEND, poor students) particularly affected; teaching to the test; a lack of critical thinking and creative opportunities.

So how do we address these issues?

By completely transforming the way we teach and learn.

Finland is in the process of moving to a whole system of cross-curricular project-based or phenomenon-based learning. Such learning brings together the acquisition of knowledge, skills and exploration in an interactive and dynamic process. Finland's Education Agency requires schools to offer at least one such project every year but with the freedom to expand further.

I have had some experience with this kind of teaching and learning when I ran a Year 7 transition project in my secondary school called Learning Competences (LC). Our team was given 20% of the Year 7 timetable and staff from across different subject areas. Together we developed a cross-curricular programme that ran for around seven years and became valued by both staff and students. We had six key projects that had exploration, creativity and independence at their root:

- *East End Icons* was an independent research project to discover the history of amazing local people which culminated in an exhibition for the local community, judged by OAPs from a local day-care centre.
- *Alien CSI* was an investigation to find out which of 12 members of staff was an alien and, as well as developing investigative skills and critical thinking, allowed us to explore what it means to be an outsider in a community.
- *Entrepreneurs* called on students to work in teams to research, devise and make a brand-new game. Each student had a specific role and developed related skills. Finalists were judge by a team of outside experts and the winners got taken to lunch in a taxi at the end of the assembly. It was a very popular project…

Other projects included *Trash to Treasure* (an exploration of art and environment which resulted in the creation of a piece of art made from rubbish) and Survival which included personal health and safety, financial skills, learning skills and two days exploring the outdoors with a sleepover.

We also ran short courses where students worked to develop a particular skill. Over the years we ran a huge range of courses including football coaching, website-building, campaign groups, art and animation projects, publishing initiatives (including poetry and a newspaper), community and fundraising events such as summer fairs.

One group worked with a gardener and garden designer to create two roof gardenspaces: one a reflective Arabic garden; the other a productive fruit and vegetable garden. The spaces were officially opened with a lunch for all involved made by food technology students using produce from the garden.

The energy and enthusiasm for learning was infectious and it spread to other areas. The school library became an important hub for students and the staff worked hard to provide good resources and training on research skills. The Library reading clubs staged ambitious events including a school-based version of the Hunger Games and a Harry Potter competition complete with costume and props. When we were reading Warhorse, one very enthusiastic member of staff arranged for a horse to come to school.

Hundreds of young people took part in these events in their own time because they wanted to and because it was learning they found exciting.

So, what happened?

The pressure for the school to hit its attainment targets for OFSTED meant the school became anxious about giving so much Y7 time to projects like this, despite both internal and external evaluations showing their value to learning and pupil engagement. Funding cuts meant a drastic reduction in library staff and resources so that now we have one member of staff where we used to have three. The Library is still the heart and soul of the school but there is no capacity for such events anymore.

It was clear that students who took part in LC gained so much. The students said they liked 'having choices', 'getting out and about', 'working in groups' and 'being creative'. When the project closed, one girl told me she felt sorry for her sister because she would never get the chance to do all the things she had. Parental feedback was also supportive with parents commenting on an increased enthusiasm for independent learning and the skills students had learned as part of working in teams.

But perhaps the words of one of the long-standing members of the team best sums up what a project-based curriculum did for teaching and learning:

> *"A fantastic teaching experience that challenged me as a teacher and the kids I taught. It allowed me to think out of the box and work with teachers from different departments and collaborate on good practice and pedagogy. A dynamic experience – nothing was repeated. We had a robust and democratic evaluation system bringing in students, parents and teachers. It was really exciting. There was a buzz in the room. It had that rare ability to enfranchise everyone from the confident high ability kids, to the shy kids that needed to come out of their shells. Its impact was beyond y7 and our subject."*

It was the most profound teaching experience of my career. Nothing I have done since has come close and I wish I had fought harder to stop its demise.

But my school is not the only one that has tried hard to fight free of the straightjacket of the Exam Factory. Up and down the country, in spite of significant constraints, educators are attempting to create exciting and challenging lessons. Classroom staff and activists have been key in establishing initiatives like Northern Rocks, Decolonising the Curriculum, Challenging Sexism, Education for the Future: Climate Emergency and Celebrating Education. All have run big successful conferences to inform, educate and enthuse. Many educators are trying to put these ideas into practice.

But imagine what we could do if we were really free to innovate and create? Imagine if decolonising the curriculum didn't rely on a small number of committed staff but instead was at the heart of the system. Imagine if that system wasn't forced to dance to the tune of OFSTED. Imagine if we had the money and resources to employ and train staff in more collaborative ways of working – and the money to buy experiences for all our children like trips to the theatre and residentials in the country or even another country. Imagine if we had the money to fund and resource our schools properly.

We do now have a chance to think again about what and how we are teaching and learning. We should take it. We should ask hard questions of ourselves and the system. We should demand more for our young people. We will need to work together to find answers.

Education in this country was not meeting the needs of the world we knew before Covid-19.

But now the world has changed.

Education will need to change as well.

Kiri Tunks

Black lives matter, anti-racist education and decolonising the curriculum

O N 25 MAY 2020, George Floyd, a 46 year old Black American man was killed by police in Minneapolis. His murder sparked a global outcry against the endemic racism in our societies. Huge Black Lives Matters protests took place with large numbers of young people attending.

In Bristol during one of these protests a statue of Edward Colston was toppled and plunged into the harbour.

Daniel Kebede, senior vice president elect of the NEU, wrote an article following this for the Independent https://www.indy100.com/article/edward-colston-statue-bristol-slavery-education-schools-black-lives-matter-9557141

He rightly points out that most people would have had no idea who Colston was however the toppling of his statue *'taught people more about slavery than UK schools ever will – unless we decolonise education'.*

Decolonising the curriculum was something that the Union had been working on prior to the covid19 crisis. However, the crisis has exposed the massive inequalities that exist in the UK and needed focused work to support our members and communities and challenge the government rhetoric.

Daniel Kebede below reports on the work that the NEU did in facing these challenges.

"There have been three main areas of work:

Our response to Covid19

The NEU hosted a weekly "Check-in" meeting for Black members. Over 200 black educators routinely attend to share their experiences and have questions answered.

A Covid19 Focus Group of 12 black educators was organised to meet with the NEU leadership and input into the union response in regards to black members.

The Union has produced advice and guidance –

● 10 Points – what you need to know about racial disparities and Covid 19 here:
https://neu.org.uk/coronavirus-what-you-need-know-racial-disparities-covid-19
● Corona Virus and Black educators frequently asked questions here:
https://neu.org.uk/advice/coronavirus-faqs-black-educators
● Guidance for staff who are higher risk outlined here:
https://neu.org.uk/advice/coronavirus-neu-advice-medically-vulnerable-and-higher-risk-groups

NEU calls on government to develop advice on the issues of greater health risk outlined in the Fenton review here:
https://neu.org.uk/press-releases/fenton-review-covid-19

5 tests on reopening schools

national education union

"Teachers, parents and staff have responded with the utmost seriousness and professionalism to the Covid-19 crisis. They need to be confident that public health is the first priority in all considerations concerning how we move forward and together combat this terrible virus. If confidence and clarity are lacking, there is a risk of chaos and greater spread of the virus."
Mary Bousted (NEU joint General Secretary)

Five tests

We want to begin to re-open schools and colleges as soon as we can. But this needs to be safe for society, for children and their families and the staff who work in them.

We have these five tests which the Government should show will be met by reliable evidence, peer-reviewed science and transparent decision-making.

Test 1

Much lower numbers of Covid-19 cases

The new case count must be much lower than it is now, with a sustained downward trend, with confidence that new cases are known and counted promptly. And the Government must have extensive arrangements for testing and contact tracing to keep it that way.

Test 2

A national plan for social distancing

The government must have a national plan including parameters for both appropriate physical distancing and levels of social mixing in schools, as well as for appropriate PPE, which will be locally negotiated at school-by-school and local authority level.

Test 3

Testing, testing, testing!

Comprehensive access to regular testing for children and staff to ensure our schools and colleges don't become hot spots for Covid-19.

Test 4

A whole school strategy

Protocols to be put in place to test a whole school or college when a case occurs and for isolation to be strictly followed.

Test 5

Protection for the vulnerable

Vulnerable staff, and staff who live with vulnerable people, must work from home, fulfilling their professional duties to the extent that is possible. Plans must specifically address the protection of vulnerable parents, grandparents and carers.

Join the NEU: www.neu.org/join

National recovery plan for education

national education union

1 Disadvantaged children and young people – and their families – must be a key priority. They must not become casualties of Covid-19.

2 Free school meals must be provided over the summer holidays so that disadvantaged children do not go hungry. Holiday hunger was real pre-Covid-19 – it will be worse this summer.

3 Local authorities must be funded to make a summer holiday offer to children and young people. They should coordinate the planning of summer holiday clubs, particularly in areas of deprivation, so that children and young people have a safe place to go to and positive activities to engage and interest them. This will help build their confidence for a successful return to school in September. Places for those on Free School Meals should be fully funded by Government.

4 Public buildings, such as libraries and sports halls, civic centres and religious buildings, should be used to expand the space available to schools so that social distancing can be achieved, with greater numbers of pupils being educated in non-school settings, if not in schools.

5 Qualified teachers who have left the profession should be encouraged to return to teaching. They will be needed as class sizes will be smaller. This will help all children who have gone through a traumatic time during the crisis and, in particular, disadvantaged children who will benefit greatly from lower pupil/teacher ratios.

6 GCSE and A levels must be changed to provide a fair assessment of young people's attainment. Exams cannot be expected to cover all the current syllabus because of the reduced teaching time. Proposals could involve a combination of teacher assessment and slimmed-down exams, with more choice of questions. Whatever the decisions made, teachers, pupils and their parents need to know that the emergency measures adopted for GCSE and A level exams in 2020 will not be repeated in 2021. Government needs to reassure all those involved that this will be a fair process that will not disadvantage young people and their futures. Primary SATs should not take place – they are mainly a school accountability measure and will not be comparable to previous or subsequent years.

7 Plans must be made for blended learning – pupils learning at school and at home – from September and into the next academic year, with all pupils having both face-to-face contact and remote learning when this is safe. These plans will be needed in case of a second spike or a rise in a local R rate. This must be resourced by Government and teachers supported to develop blended learning as has happened in Scotland.

8 Children and young people living in poverty and low-income households must be given the resources they need to learn at home, including access to books and creative resources, as well as technology. Seven hundred thousand children live in homes without internet access. This must be provided by Government so that they are able to access on-line learning. Free laptops must be provided for children who do not have them so that they are able to access online learning at home.

9 Childhood poverty and inequality limits life chances and is a significant factor in school achievement. We must not lose a generation because the pandemic makes even more children poor. This requires a 'can do' mentality – around unemployment, training and benefits as well as direct support to schools.

10 A fully resourced national plan for children's wellbeing should be launched to support children who suffered trauma in the pandemic. Students' wellbeing must be placed at the centre of how we adapt education to meet the needs of children and young people.

Coronavirus crisis

NEU1903/0620

'We can't go back to doing things the same way'

Trauma

When schools closed their doors to most children at the end of March, school leaders and staff were quick to adapt to making alternative arrangements for their pupils.

In the absence of any coherent government guidance, full credit must go to those educators who by the following Monday morning had established emergency plans for continuing a teaching and learning dialogue between homes and schools in an effort to ensure that no child would miss out.

Additionally, it was the turn of parents and carers to bring out their inner teacher and convert dining tables and kitchens into makeshift classrooms and any available outdoor space into mini PE areas. Children who couldn't access yards or gardens had the effervescent Joe Wicks to help them burn off some excess energy.

Unfortunately, this wasn't the picture for all children and families and those who did manage to establish a timetable of sorts for at-home lessons soon discovered that distance learning is no replacement for the myriad opportunities that school settings offer.

Many schools have reported a low uptake of online learning, unsurprising as many thousands of children in the UK currently live in homes without internet access. (Free Broadband for all, anyone…?)

Of those homes that do have access many are 'device poor' and do not have the tablets or laptops to support the online learning of two or more children simultaneously, as well as any adults attempting to work from home.

Instead, many families took to a blended approach of formal teaching, play and child-led learning activities that worked for them and was facilitated by a wealth of resources, both online and paper, which have been provided free of charge by schools and a range of other outlets during lockdown.

Following the announcement that there would be no formal testing for pupils this summer, educators and families could heave a sigh of relief and focus more on the emotional needs of their children rather than the revision sessions, the booster groups and the practice papers that usually dominate school spring calendars in the UK.

In the absence of thirty, sixty or more books to mark each night, teachers were now delivering distance learning and then making phone calls to families to check on their welfare and see how they were coping with the 'new normal'.

The default position became one of nurture, support and practical help; thousands of emergency food parcels were delivered by school staff to homes during the lockdown. As millions took to displaying rainbows on windows as symbols of hope and standing on doorsteps applauding care workers there was a refreshing sense of community in the air.

Of course, schools have always played a vital role in attending to the pastoral needs of children and families. Not least since 2010 when drastic austerity measures were introduced by the Conservative and Liberal Democrat Coalition government. During the following years the impact on families was severe, as detailed in UNICEF's 2017 report 'Children of Austerity':

"Households with children were some of the main victims of austerity…

The Coalition government had promised fairness in its deficit-reduction strategy, but low-income families with children were hit hard."

This headline from *The Telegraph* in April 2018 – "Teachers are having to wash children's clothes and lend their parents money" – is testament to the situation many schools found themselves in.

Transition

It is against this backdrop of swingeing spending cuts that COVID 19 spread across the globe in a pandemic not seen since the devastating and deadly flu virus of 1918.

As we begin a wider re-opening of schools, educators, parents and children are wondering what education will be like in our new, sanitised and socially distanced world. We're beginning to see how schools will appear: sparser, definitely; austere and unwelcoming, possibly.

The single desks with spaces in between for even the youngest children are reminiscent of Victorian Sunday schools. Resources will be limited, playthings restricted and all soft furnishings removed completely. Even books will have to be carefully rationed for fear of contamination.

But what schools will be depends largely on the people in them. The pandemic has given pause for thought. Schools have been forced to step back and we shouldn't rush or be pushed into trying to return to things as they were.

As educators and parents we need to decide what we want our children to return to. We need to examine what it is about education that we most value. What does it mean to leave a child 'behind'? Behind what or whom? Since all children learn at their own pace then they will inevitably need to readjust at their own pace too. Should passing tests and exams really be the ultimate goal of education? It has seemed that way for years.

These things are important of course, but is it too much of a 'one size fits all' approach. One size doesn't fit all. It never did. Isn't it time we were able to not only acknowledge children's mental health needs, for example, but prioritise them?

For too long the supposedly 'broad and balanced' National Curriculum has been slowly shrinking to accommodate an education methodology driven by data, results and league tables. In this context, you may have already heard of another 'GERM' infecting schools around the world: the Global Education Reform Movement.

Numeracy and literacy are essential skills of course, but have been given undue emphasis at the expense of the arts, sciences, humanities and sports, despite it being well documented that these foundation subjects play a vital role in developing children's interests, minds and bodies. It's an unhealthy trend and we should not pursue it any longer.

This pause is a golden opportunity to reassess what should be 'non-negotiable' about education. Tests for four year olds, phonics screening, SATs and GCSEs are all up for scrutiny and must be reassessed. There are lessons to be learned. Will we be able to emerge from this crisis renewed and re-invigorated with a state education system that is fit for purpose for all its people?

The National Education Union has been at the forefront of the campaign for a return to schools only when it is safe. Last week the NEU forced the Government to finally accept that expecting all primary school pupils to return to school for a month before the summer break was simply not safe.

On 11 June the NEU published an open letter to the prime minister outlining its proposals for a ten-point National Education Recovery Plan, beginning over the summer holidays and addressing the needs of all children and young people with a particular focus on children from disadvantaged backgrounds.

Additionally, the NEU has produced further guidance for educators on a way forward in the summer term. It is based on five key principles and for use whether children are learning at home or at school and comprises 'Five Cs' that could help to shape the teaching and learning in the immediate aftermath of the return and hopefully beyond.

The following, in italics, is taken directly from the NEU guidance, with permission:

Focus on Caring
Caring about the wellbeing of pupils, families and staff needs to be the primary focus. Schools and colleges are social institutions which play a role at the heart of their community. The Government has highlighted particular groups of children as 'vulnerable', but many children may face abuse, isolation, friendship troubles, poor mental health, hunger, bullying and exploitation during this unusual term.

Focus on the Context for learning
This is not education as normal. We believe schools' goal during this time must be to keep students connected to a range of learning, by making sure that learning is relevant and based on students' experience. Evidence from education in emergency zones shows starting from students' individual needs and experiences is what works. We are asking the Department for Education (DfE) to create a transitional phase, which could remain in place for longer than anticipated. In this period, learning must be realistic, taking into account that teachers have children at home with them and many parent/carers are working, not 'home-schooling' their children.

Focus on a Creative curriculum
Using the summer term to let pupils create, make and perform projects that interest them can provide opportunities for students to express their feelings and emotions, spark their imagination, develop independence, maintain motivation and build resilience in the face of uncertainty.

Focus on Connecting
Creating drawings, lists, plans or homemade postcards can connect children to neighbours, relatives or friends and keep that connection. Include a Covid Time Capsule to help students creatively chart their experiences.

Focus on building and celebrating your Community

Research shows that it will really help students to develop resilience if they feel that they are making a positive difference, are trusted and viewed as responsible – whether that is helping in their home, helping with younger siblings, or helping people in their street/estate/area. Make sure your school validates this use of time and this contribution or informal care which students might be making within their home, or in the community around them. Activities such as putting up posters in the window, or making care packages for neighbours, have benefits for both learning and wellbeing and should be celebrated and validated.

Transformation

The ten-point plan and the 'Five Cs' advocate child and family-centred approaches and start with where the children are. We cannot, must not, ignore the national trauma of the last few months. We will need to face it before we can possibly move on. Children – and adults – will need to process their experiences and will need time to adjust.

Many children will have gone through bereavement; all children will have gone through some form of loss. There must be no return to 'business as usual' and only when we have addressed that loss can we hope to rebuild. We need not return to the 'exam factory' conditions that previously determined the school experiences of our children. Just as the forest rejuvenates after the drama and destruction of a wildfire, so must we nurture the shoots of recovery. How we shape that renewal is up to us.

Karen Parkin

Supporting learning in the summer term

This document is a framework for supporting the continuation of learning for students.

Summer term learning during COVID-19 should be focussed on 5 key principles, whether children and young people are learning at home or in school.

We need to focus on:-

CARE
CONTEXT
CREATE
CONNECT
COMMUNITY

A. Focus on Caring

Caring about the wellbeing of pupils, families and staff needs to be the primary focus. Schools and colleges are social institutions which play a role at the heart of their community. The Government has highlighted particular groups of children as 'vulnerable', but many children may face abuse, isolation, friendship troubles, poor mental health, hunger, bullying and exploitation during this unusual term. For NEU guidance on vulnerable children, see here.

Physical health and wellbeing: Many families will face increased financial and social challenges during this time. Ensuring families have access to support, including free school meals, food banks, and other services, is critical to meeting basic needs. It is as important to provide families with links and encourage them to do physical activities as it is to set academic work.

Mental and emotional wellbeing: This is a stressful time for many, with bereavement, chaos, social issues, loss of familiar routines, isolation and other issues impacting on pupil mental health and wellbeing. Supporting the development of reassuring environments, providing learning resources on COVID-19, mental health and general wellbeing, and supporting those conversations to happen within families, are central aspects of education at the moment. For more on supporting pupils' mental health, see here.

The emotional health and wellbeing of education staff must be protected for them to support families. School leaders and mental health leads should work with unions and staff to develop plans to protect staff health and wellbeing, and to work out what it is realistic for staff to juggle. These plans should include regular breaks, flexible working for those with caring responsibilities and regular signposting to counselling and mental health services. All vulnerable staff and pregnant women must work from home.

Tailored care: All pupils need contact and support through this time, and this should be tailored as far as possible to what they need. Schools know that children approaching key transitions will need specific messages of reassurance and emotional support. The support offered to children with a social worker, to children with special educational needs and to other vulnerable children, should be co-ordinated and agreed with the child, their parents/carers and the local authority where appropriate. For more on external support services, see here.

B. Focus on the Context for learning

This is not education as normal. **We believe schools' goal during this time must be to keep students connected to a range of learning, by making sure that learning is relevant and based on students' experience. Evidence from education in emergency zones shows starting from students' individual needs and experiences is what works. We are asking the Department for Education (DfE) to create a transitional phase, which could remain in place for longer than anticipated. In this period, learning must be realistic, taking into account that teachers have children at home with them and many parent/carers are working, not 'home-schooling' their children.**

Reassure parents: Being clear with students and families about what is expected of them and what the school is able to provide will help everyone feel more in control and less stressed by the current uncertainty. Teaching children at home is not the job of parents/carers, supporting children's learning is an additional responsibility. Teaching is a highly skilled role and, while some parent/carers will feel quite confident in supporting their children's learning, many will not be able to do this. The NEU recognises that a large proportion of independent (fee paying) schools are operating a near full timetable of lessons, where full participation is expected. While this is not possible for all of their pupils, we are providing support for our members in those schools and have provided further guidance <u>here</u>.

Consolidation is the goal: It is hugely valuable for schools to support students to develop habits of learning at home in a way that consolidates learning and reinforces existing content and understanding. We do not want pupils to worry about learning or about progress they think others are making. Instead they should be reassured that as we get back to a new normal after the transition phase, their school will help them to adjust. Teachers and support staff should think of and frame distance learning as an opportunity for pupils to work independently or in small groups, on things they are familiar with and gently introduce some new ideas.

Language matters: References to "missed work" or "lost time" or "catch up" will increase anxiety. For as many as half your pupils, any independent working will be extremely challenging or impossible. Instead, consolidated learning could include, for example, quizzes and extension challenges on humanities topics learned before lockdown, such as Vikings or rivers; practice questions, extension challenges and practical application of maths work already taught, such as fractions, length, time; or reading other books by an author read in class, making comparisons of themes, characters and so on.

Realistic approach to assessment: When a teacher gives a pupil formative feedback on classwork, they know and understand the learning that led to that piece of work and the circumstances in which it was done. This is not the case for work done at home. Older children may receive more feedback on work from their subject teachers, where appropriate, but this needs to be kept proportionate to the teacher's circumstances and the work being done. Feedback should generally be short, supportive and encouraging. It does not need to be daily, or even weekly. Other communication, such as general praise for engagement in schoolwork, opportunities to share other activities, encouragement, etc. is just as important.

Iterative process: This is a period of emergency, which means we need to enable teachers to focus on positive relationships with students and attempting reasonable routines, rather than making linear progress. It will help teachers to seek feedback from parents/carers and students and adjust their practice in response, where appropriate. For most teachers and pupils in state-funded schools, a full programme of distance teaching and learning has been shown to be unrealistic and too complex. The Sutton Trust has found that most children are not accessing learning or returning work set by schools. To forge ahead in this manner is to ignore the reality of how challenging it is for students to find the motivation, space or equipment to study at home day in, day out.

C. Focus on a Creative curriculum

Using the summer term to let pupils create, make and perform projects that interest them can provide opportunities for students to express their feelings and emotions, spark their imagination, develop independence, maintain motivation and build resilience in the face of uncertainty.

Creative projects: There are a range of ways that schools can support pupils to learn through making and creating. For example, baking and cooking provide opportunities to talk about science (materials - changing states and senses – taste). For those with a garden, allotment or balcony, there are opportunities for planting seeds, understanding how plants grow, identifying plants and insects, and drawing plants. Making music doesn't necessarily require traditional instruments. Children can be challenged to make an instrument out of recycled materials, compose a musical score and create a performance.

Support social and emotional needs through creativity: Creative projects support children and young people's social and emotional needs and will help them to process the current worrying and disorienting situation. Examples of this kind of learning are provided in the **AGENDA toolkit** with activities like **What jars you?**, getting children to 'felt' their feelings, create mood boards or make a relationships web.

Reading challenges: Encouraging students to use the time to read for pleasure is not straightforward but is worth the effort, because it is transformative for resilience and triggers success in all areas of learning. Reading is shown to help students make sense of their anxiety and worry, and can counteract excessive screen time. The NEU has worked with education expert Debra Kidd to produce free **creative reading packs** that schools can use with parents and children from Reception to Year 6. You can also check out the **UKLA,** **Book Trust** and **Penguin** for ideas on books and **poetry** for older and more advanced readers.

D. Focus on Connecting

Creating drawings, lists, plans or homemade postcards can connect children to neighbours, relatives or friends and keep that connection. Include some prompts in your home learning packs. Include the <u>Covid Time Capsule</u> to help students creatively chart their experiences (suitable for primary and secondary).

Stay in touch: Don't underestimate how helpful a school newsletter or subject weekly email can be. Many students feel lonely and disorientated and miss the rhythms of school. Levels of communication need to be realistic for staff, and students will have different reactions - some will worry that they want to get the work done and some will feel very unmotivated. Online platforms and printed home learning packs provide a structure, but staff do not need to follow the normal curriculum or aim to push students through the content at a 'normal' pace.

Pupils with peers: Many pupils will be missing their peers. Facilitating calls and assigning projects to be worked on together or in pairs will maintain social and learning relationships. Creating fun activities or book reviews for students to discuss with each other can keep that connection and engagement.

Younger pupils: Connecting younger pupils with online assemblies, or setting students online challenges to do at home and getting them to send back pictures of the results, helps childrn share their work and stay connected. Creating pictures and writing letters, and either dropping them into the school letter box or uploading and emailing them, is a fun way for pupils to engage with their teachers.

Exam groups: Exams will not be taking place this summer as we know it. Pupils who were scheduled to sit GCSE, A-level or AS-level exams now find themselves in a very different place academically and emotionally, as those exams have been cancelled. Those pupils can still be engaged in learning, in extension projects to consolidate their learning, and opportunities to think about what they will be doing next. Exam groups are a positive support network connecting pupils going through the same experiences and emotions. More guidance on exams can be found **here**.

E. Focus on building and celebrating your Community

A sense of agency and belonging for students: Research shows that it will really help students to develop resilience if they feel that they are making a positive difference, are trusted and viewed as responsible - whether that is helping in their home, helping with younger siblings, or helping people in their street/estate/area. Make sure your school validates this use of time and this contribution or informal care which students might be making within their home, or in the community around them. Activities such as putting up posters in the window, or making care packages for neighbours, have benefits for both learning and wellbeing and should be celebrated and validated.

Supporting families: The NEU has developed a **parent microsite** to support families through this unusual term. The NEU has also produced a **model poster** for your school to use with families to publicise helplines and national sources of information about mental health, domestic violence and other challenges.

Supporting the community: The NEU is recommending that schools put together free **Create Boxes** to send home for children who might not have creative supplies available. What could students create for their neighbourhood? What art activities could your school community do together, to still feel connected? Could students drop posters in to display on the school gates? Could students decorate stones or tiles with what they are missing?

Community of professionals: As a professional learning community, staff need the opportunity to talk about what training and professional development would help them to respond to the new challenges. Trauma informed approaches? Online skills? Reading for pleasure? Although there are multiple short-term challenges, this is not the time to give up on CPD. Your NEU union group should identify what CPD is the priority to support you to adjust the curriculum, refresh assessment skills and respond to the social and emotional needs of your students. Your school will need to build its capacity to respond to children's emotional and learning needs, and to manage the transition phase when it comes - this needs to be a collective discussion.

Support for all school staff: NQTs, trainees, cleaners, school nurses, food preparation workers and supply teachers are all key workers. All school staff need support. As a school team you will know the particular needs of your colleagues, and your **union rep** will be able to support members where necessary. The NEU expects **exceptional treatment** to be given this year for those on initial teacher training, with those on course to gain QTS receiving it. The NEU has also called on schools to **continue paying supply educators** until the end of their engagement and to maintain contracts, including those agreed but not yet started. The NEU encourages schools to support all their workers, regardless of their role or activity level, at this time.

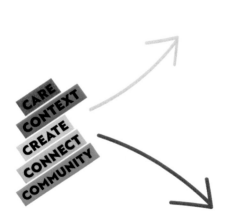

SEND Now

IN 2019, a 'SEND Crisis' was declared. After years of crippling cuts to education, including a 1.7 billion pound shortfall to SEND funding and poor central government implementation of SEND reforms, local authorities struggled to work within their high needs budget and support schools with fulfilling Educational Health Care Plan (EHCP) requirements. Since the beginning of school partial closure due to COVID19, SEND once again has proven to be an afterthought for the Conservatives. After weeks of uncertainty about going in to lock down and even more dithering about whether or not to implement school closures, the 18th March finally saw the government announce that schools would close to pupils 'except those whose parents were key workers and those with Educational Health Care Plans'.

Rightly so there was a flurry of questions from parents/carers and educationalists. 'Is it mandatory to send my child in? ', 'If I work in a SEND provision are we still open as all our children have ECHPs?', 'Are there no more specific guidelines for SEND provisions?' Quite frankly, as an experienced SEND specialist, the question I was asking was 'Does Boris Johnson, Gavin Williamson or any of the Tory party know what an EHCP plan is or what a special school actually looks like? We all know the answer to that one. It goes without saying that within the Etonian bubble that terms such as PMLD (profound and multiple learning disabilities), SLD (severe learning disability), SEMH (social, emotional and mental health), SpLD (specific learning difference) and Pupil Referral Units are just a mixture of letters that mean absolutely nothing. I know that one SEND school within my borough, due to such dithering from the government and concern re the safety of their staff and pupils partially closed their school the week before any announcement was made in regards to school closures.

As a member of a senior leadership team (SLT), keeping up to speed with government guidelines for education during COVID19 has been extremely difficult to say the least, especially when having to interpret and adapt school policy for those pupils with additional and complex needs. Announcements have been made with minimal thought and then had to be clarified and tweaked days after. At one point the government guidelines were changed forty times – this is beyond farcical when trying to communicate with parents and staff and make decisions about pupil and staff well-being and safety. This poor level of thought and communication from central government meant that in some SEND schools the majority of pupils were sent into school despite the fact, it was not compulsory and that they were much safer at home.

Working in any kind of SEND provision whether it is SEMH or SLD/ASC/PMLD based, is extremely complex. There are many needs to take into consideration – personal care, managing extreme and challenging behaviour, communication and sensory needs to name but a few. The majority of pupils need a high level of adult support in addition to using a higher level of practical and supporting resources such as PECS symbols, sensory apparatus, physical apparatus to support physical needs and practical apparatus to support learning. This has added to the complexity and time needed to ensure thorough and well thought out risk assessments are in place. Not to mention that the needs of some individuals have meant further individual risk assessments have been needed.

All this has been carried out well by SEND schools despite the fact there has been little to no guidance from central government which has essentially surmounted to a tokenistic 'look after vulnerable pupils' and 'SEND provisions do what you need to, it doesn't have to be quite the same as mainstream'. As an experienced educationalist, I would normally welcome a lack of interference from politicians, especially a Conservative one but such an unusual situation as COVID19 requires a more holistic, cohesive approach that can't be left solely to a school's SLT in a couple of Zoom meetings. The obvious example that the government should have followed would be Denmark where the government consulted and worked with the teaching unions to provide a well thought out and safe plan to reopen schools.

It is worth noting how much responsibility the Conservative party has heaped on Local Authorities during this time, the same Local Authorities they have systemically decimated for the last decade and left with huge deficits in budgets. Many SEMH provisions don't even come under an authority anymore, as like my school, they are an independent establishment funded by multiple local authorities.

The indecisive incoherent, blanket approach taken by this Tory government has put unsurmountable pressure and stress on all schools but none more so than SEND ones. In fact, when the R rate rose in the North West above 1 again just a few days before we were due to start phasing children back into school, many LAs and schools had to amend or scrap previous plans. Plans that took a lot of hard work to put together. Having to change plans last minute has a big impact on pupils such as ours who thrive with routine and being around key adults and a highly tailored setting and who struggle enormously with change.

Social distancing of two metres has been key in dealing with COVID19, maintaining this in any schools or educational setting is extremely difficult due to the social nature of them. Maintaining this in SEND settings is another matter. Social stories and marked tape aside, many pupils with complex needs struggle with the concept of the space and needing to distance – some are just not physically able to do so. For those pupils with personal care and physical/medical needs, two adults are often needed, such acts of care can't take place without being close to the pupil.

Similarly, in most SEMH provisions, physical intervention namely TEAM TEACH is used as a last resort for when pupils become a danger to themselves and others. How and if to use such programmes has been a big factor to consider and of course, form part of risk assessments. I know within my own school, staff anxiety around such issues has been heightened.

Positive relationships are key to working in any area of education and none more so than in SEND. Relationships can often be quite tactile and to many children with SEND, having key known adults is vital to their routine and emotional well-being. Thank goodness for technology is all I can say! Digital meetings whilst limited, have at least meant that some interaction has taken place. I know for our pupils who were in during partial closures and for those who have returned to school, not being able to hug staff or have the same level of sensory intervention has been challenging for them.

SEND schools have done an excellent job in the outreach they have provided whilst school have been partially closed. Like our mainstream counterparts, the differentiated work packs have gone home where appropriate, creative projects have been set and a high level of pastoral support has been put in place. Alongside the SEND schools I work with and the number I follow on social media and the like, it has been heartening to see all the baking, planting and creativity taking place at home. As to be expected, our baking and gardening packs that our school has sent out to pupils have been significantly better received than the more formal work packs.

It is worth bearing in mind, that all this positive work undertaken during difficult circumstances has taken place under a government that has been clearly making it up as they go along.

Naomi Fearon

A radical vision for a new 14-19 curriculum

Why 14 to 19?

We must rethink the foundations of upper-secondary education as the current system is so fractured and incoherent that it undercuts the potential of institutions and individual young people alike. We must look to build an educational system that England's young people need and deserve. This requires Government to have a clearer vision of the upper secondary phase, with a consistently broader curriculum and more coherent approaches to funding, institutional choice and accountability across the age range.[1]

IN 2010, the age when learners could legally leave education or training was raised to 18. This was a result of a previous Labour Education Act (2008) which would have been too embarrassing for the Tories to reverse. Despite the change in the law, the incoming Tory government made no changes to the way curriculum and assessment operated. Nothing was done to integrate Key Stage 4 into the upper secondary phase and GCSEs were maintained as a selective gateway to advanced study. Also, Michael Gove cut the Education Maintenance Allowance and at the same time invested little in trying to keep learners from dropping off the radar. A result is that nine per cent of learners effectively disappear from education aged 16, despite the statutory raising of the age.

Vocational courses are rarely positive choices for learners post-16. There are a number of vocational qualifications which count in performance tables available to learners below the age of 16. However, the Progress 8 measure and pressure from government for more learners to take the EBAC mean that learners have to be seen to fluff their more academic GCSEs before they can start an in-depth vocational course of study. Equivalence between vocational and academic courses has never been at such a low level. Vocational courses are taken because learners fail to get good enough grades to follow A level courses. The separation between the vocational and academic will be even more strongly delineated with the advent of the new T levels, which will prevent learners from taking a combination of vocational and academic courses post-16.

Upper secondary school education where learners can choose courses appropriate to destinations beyond further education, effectively lasts two years in England. Funding for a third year of study which supports disadvantaged learners in reaching higher education and higher apprenticeships has been savagely cut by the Tories by nearly 20 per cent. There is a mix of approaches across Europe. Thirteen countries start their upper secondary phase below the age of 16 and only Spain, along with the UK, has a two-year upper secondary phase.

A bigger, broader and more meaningful curriculum with a spine of genuine skills[2] for learning and life for the post-14 cohort, is a longstanding aim of progressive educationalists. It makes sense for the UK, in which a considerable amount of work has already been carried out to establish a 14 -19 phase in curriculum terms, notably the Tomlinson report in 2004, to move towards this mode[3]. This would allow equivalence between the academic and vocational throughout the phase, a common core for all learners, together with increasing choice as they progress through it, encompassing either academic, vocational courses or a mix of the two. This would be a four-year programme for most learners, but a fifth fully funded year available for learners who need it. GCSE would become no more than a progress check.

A radical new curriculum

14-19 curricula have been riddled with re-inventions since the advent of YTS in the 1980s and before, but its emphasis on 'common', 'core', 'key' or 'essential' skills has played a significant part in the personal learning and employability potential of many learners during that time and has provided a foot on the ladder of employability. A mechanistic basic skills version of skills' development is once again in the ascendancy. A fuller, more developmental model of skills-retrieving aspects of the softer key skills developed in the noughties, comprising improving own learning, working with others and problem-solving, is as important as ever in a progressive 14-19 curriculum.

We on the left need to keep faith with this braver 14-19 curriculum so that a future Labour government can commit to radical curriculum reform and introduce a National Education Service (NES) championed by its advisers, teachers and researchers. This means implementing, in the 14-19 phase, a unified developmental curriculum where the academic and vocational are equally valued. At its heart, it should be developing the skills and knowledge in our young people, necessary to engage fully with the modern world in a critical and reflective way. Communication in all its facets, problem-solving, collaboration, critical thinking and reflection must feature. It must also be flexible and personalised, allowing young people to choose courses which suit their aspirations and interests. Finally, the assessment model should recognise the achievements of all learners, including those with special educational needs (SENDs), rather than segregate them through crude pass/fail measures. We have been close to achieving the above on occasion, notably the Tomlinson reforms proposed in 2004 and the short lived curriculum 2000 agenda.

A progressive 14-19 curriculum must:

• develop the knowledge, skills, attitudes and dispositions to enable young people to be responsible citizens and independent thinkers. Learners should be prepared for employment, competent to make choices and learn throughout their lives.

• prepare 19 year-olds to progress to employment or continue in education, with useful social and learning skills and qualifications that are valuable and understood by both employers and education institutions;

• be sufficiently engaging to retain young people at risk of leaving education, employment and training. [5]

Comprehensive and Inclusive

Our arguments for a comprehensive approach which maintains a common curriculum (and for that matter minimises grouping by 'ability') until upper secondary, where students should have a significant degree of choice over the combination of courses they take, are backed up by the OECD Report: Equity and Quality in Education: Supporting Disadvantaged Students and Schools (2012). This report identifies the characteristics of education systems which do best by disadvantaged learners. One characteristic is delaying 'tracking' (in the English system streaming or differentiating the curriculum) until the upper secondary phase and a second is providing equivalent pathways which enables transfer between them.

In the UK despite the skills shortage in a range of areas the stratification of pathways means that 70 per cent of learners in upper secondary are taking general/academic education courses. There is an urgent need to resource vocational education properly to make it more attractive to learners and increase quality. It also means in England, depending on learner goals and interests, allowing some degree of mixing both academic and vocational options. It should certainly mean that high achievers on vocational courses should be able to transfer across to more academic university degrees if they so choose and vice versa.

The Tomlinson agenda would have:

• revolutionised assessment reducing the number of exams taken;

• allowed for learners to take assessments when they were ready rather than at a particular age;

- allowed for learners to take either specialised vocational or academic courses, as well as a mix between the two, from age 14 effectively abolishing the vocational/academic divide once and for all;
- included all learners by recognising achievement at entry level and level one for some SEND learners
- provided a qualification framework accessible throughout life.

We believe it should be the basis or a model for any radical reform of the 14-19 phase of education because it fulfils most of the characteristics the OECD report recommends: 'The design of upper secondary is key to success in overcoming school failure'.

Reviving the 14-19 debate

Is the whole 14-19 debate dead? The Tories hope that it is. They see their system as one in which the 'brightest and best" rise to the top whilst others fail to jump assessment hurdles and then pursue what the Tories perceive to be second rate courses and pathways. A levels remain the traditional 'gold standard'. Gove *et al* saw the tinkering with them by New Labour under the Curriculum 2000 initiative as sacrilege. Minor modularisation of courses which increased participation post-16, was abolished. Vocational qualifications on the other hand, have never been given a chance to become embedded so that they are trusted by parents and employers. Every incoming government or secretary of state fiddles with them. CPVE, GNVQ, the Diploma, BTECs, OCR Nationals, Tech levels etc are some of the incarnations created over the years whilst A level has remained more or less constant. Little surprise then that students and parents pressure schools to allow them to take A level courses. Just as the BTEC, recently made more 'rigorous' by the Tories, is starting to gain currency from employers and higher education, the government is giving notice it will no longer be funded. Instead new untested T levels are being rushed in against civil servant advice.

The debate is not dead and the 14-19 upper secondary phase is a particularly useful way of considering the predicament the English system finds itself in. The IPPR report (Evans 2015) states .....the educational experience of a young person which starts at the beginning of Year 10 and typically lasts four years until the end of the academic year in which they turn 18. This is the period through which all young people will be expected to complete a broad, stretching and coherent programme of study, building up a collection of knowledge, skills and experience to allow them to move into a prosperous, flexible and rewarding adulthood'. Currently though the phase is in the main over assessed, stratified, narrow and not fit for the ambitions of young people growing up in the 21st century nor any potential economic models which may emerge.

Spours, Hodgson and Rogers[6] from the UCL Institute of Education in their pamphlet '14–19 education and training in England: The concept of an extended upper secondary education phase revisited' reopens the 14-19 discussion. They suggest through their 'unified approach' a phase which as well as providing choice and improving quality would also include more breadth, interdisciplinary learning and project-based work. Wary of recommending another upheaval they suggest ways of tweaking the system to move towards the Tomlinson model: increasing breadth in academic education through A levels and project work, improving the quality of vocational education and increasing collaboration between providers. We believe we can go further without too much initiative overload. Why not incorporate existing qualifications into a Tomlinson style framework? Why not move to stage not age modes of assessment? Why not abolish GCSEs as stand-alone qualifications? Why not ensure a common skills framework that overlays both academic and vocational courses? Why not build in the kind of curriculum and pedagogy which hands over more responsibility to the learner through projects like the EPQ and increasing skills development? Why not ensure SEND learners are included by reintroducing a 'climbing frame' model of assessment which recognises what learners can do rather than what they cannot? Why not end the selective nature of some institutions and sixth forms and move towards comprehensivising the whole phase?

'…the highest performing education systems across OECD countries are those that combine quality with equity. Equity in education means that personal or social circumstances such as gender, ethnic origin or family background, are not obstacles to achieving educational potential (fairness) and that all individuals reach at least a basic minimum level of skills (inclusion). In these education systems, the vast majority of students have the opportunity to attain high level skills, regardless of their own personal and socio-economic circumstances'. OECD 2012.

These are the pre-conditions for a bigger, broader and more meaningful 14-19 curriculum and qualifications framework.

Ian Duckett and James Whiting
References

1   Louise Evans , *Moving on up: Developing a strong, coherent upper secondary education system in England* IPPR 2015
2   Ian Duckett, Skills development, pedagogy and history, *Education forTomorrow* Issue 4, July, 2020
3   Ian Duckett, David Vickers and Simon Baddeley, *14-19:; an overview*, Learning and Skills Development Agency, 2007
4   Ian Duckett, Pam Tatlow and James Whiting, 'Towards a new 14¬19 curriculum', *Education Politics*, 139, September, 2019
5   Ken Spours, Ann Hodgson and Lynne Rogers, *14–19 education and training in England: The concept of an extended upper secondary education phase revisited*, UCL/Edge Foundation, 2017
6   OECD, *Equity and Quality in Education: Supporting Disadvantaged Students and Schools*, OECD Publishing 2012

Further Education finding its place
Colleges and the crisis

THERE'S NOTHING like a serious global public health crisis to remind us of the value of care, community, equality, solidarity, and co-operation and to highlight how interconnected we are, globally and locally. A crisis on this scale turns things upside down and opens up the possibilities of rapid and radical change. It's become commonplace to observe that the COVID-19 pandemic gives us an opportunity to re-evaluate what really matters. The crisis has reminded us of the positive and protective role of the state and the human value of different kinds of economic activity and given us a more connected, global view of the consequences of our actions.

England's colleges have been active in supporting people through this crisis and as we deal with the economic fallout, they will have an important role in helping people build back better. Colleges are rooted in their communities, adding value to their local area, working at the interface of education and the economy, connecting aspiration, progression, training and employment. They also help to create and nurture the web of social and economic relationships which support cohesion and collective resilience in their communities.

A misunderstood sector?

Colleges are sometime regarded as the awkward sector in the middle; neither school nor university, overlapping and struggling to be heard while other types of institution have greater political influence. But if we try to imagine an England without its colleges, the gaping hole in our social fabric could not be patched up by other types of provider, something like a college would need to be invented. It is colleges' responsiveness and versatility which are their great strengths; they often do the vital work which others can't or don't want to do. The diversity of students, of curricula and of need only strengthens the case for the college as a full-spectrum provider. Having a single college in your community can mean having an Art school, a Business school, a Science and Engineering academy, a liberal studies sixth form, a second-chance college, a special need provider, an adult education centre, a training provider and more, all in one. This comprehensive approach also means there is no incentive to steer students into any route other than what is best for them.

Another narrative is that of colleges as a 'Cinderella' sector; misunderstood, neglected and underfunded, waiting for its prince to come. This has persisted for so long that it's almost part of our identity. The legacy of under-investment and policy neglect is very real and has certainly made the sector vulnerable. However, colleges pride themselves on their adaptability and ability to pull through every crisis. There are many signs that England's network of colleges is increasingly being seen as key to economic and social recovery and progress and a forthcoming government White Paper will probably have more to say about this.

If the 'Cinderella' label implies that colleges are waiting for an external saviour, perhaps a better metaphor is to be found in another Grimm tale, the story of the dancing princesses, which was selected as the common theme for the brilliant collection 'Further Education and the twelve dancing princesses[1] edited by Maire Daley, Kevin Orr and Joel Petrie. The princesses are held captive but escape every night to dance together in a celebration of subversive innovation and collective creativity despite the oppression they face. What great role models for a long-suffering college sector full of commitment and ideas!

What is FE? Scale, range, quality and purpose

England's Further Education sector educates and trains over two million students and has a collective turnover of around £7billion, including general FE colleges, sixth form colleges, specialist institutions and adult providers. The quality is overwhelmingly good with 82 per cent of colleges judged good or outstanding at inspection.

740,000 of college students are aged 16-18, and for young people in this age group, colleges are the majority educational provider: over 60 per cent of all 16-18-year-old students in England are studying in colleges.

By any standard, FE is a highly efficient sector; however the number of colleges has fallen from 346 to 244 over the last ten years, and their average 16-18 numbers have risen to nearly 2,500 per college. At the same time, school sixth forms have increased in number by 155 over ten years and decreased in average size to under 200 students per school. 57 per cent of all school sixth forms do not meet the government's own viability threshold of 200 students to justify a new sixth form. This proliferation of small sixth forms has happened at a time of significant cuts in public funding, making such provision even less cost-effective. Colleges have been encouraged to rationalise their provision and their final year A Level cohorts are on average over three times larger than those in schools.

Rather than tackling inefficiencies, public policy for nearly a decade has encouraged the creation of new school sixth forms, mostly offering A Levels. More providers offering the same few courses often means less choice overall. We know that having many small providers in a locality can lead to a narrowing of the course offer available to local students. For example, if you live in an area where A Level provision is mainly to be found in small sixth forms, you are likely to have fewer opportunities to access to the subjects you want.

Colleges offer 264,00 apprenticeships and are also significant providers of Higher Education, delivering the majority of Foundation Degrees and National Diplomas with a total of 137,000 HE students choosing to study at college rather than university. Last year's Augar review into post-18 education recommended a rebalancing between FE and HE and the development of a strong, higher technical route and the proposal to give colleges a stronger role in delivering 'sub-degree' courses may yet find its way into government policy.

At a time when there is a danger of Britain turning inwards, many colleges also recruit internationally and are very active in Erasmus mobility programmes with 17,000 placements in the current cycle, creating brilliant opportunities for students to see the benefits of cross-cultural learning and international cooperation.

Colleges educating the 'disadvantaged'

Colleges are key institutions in the emancipation of working-class, Black, Asian and minority ethnic students as well as for broader community development. They work with the most disadvantaged; the very people who have been disproportionately hit by the economic and health crises.

The widening achievement gap from five to 16 is well documented and post-16 it is colleges which do most of the heavy lifting in terms of narrowing that gap. For example, the overwhelming majority of all 16-18 students who hadn't achieved a grade 4 or above in GCSE English or Maths at age 16 are in colleges: 96 per cent and 92 per cent respectively. The subsequent success of 17 and 18 year-olds in improving their English and Maths is almost entirely down to the work colleges do to re-engage and re-motivate students who have struggled at school.

If we look at where the most disadvantaged 16-18 year-old students in England are studying, as defined by Free School Meal eligibility, we see that nearly three quarters are in colleges. There are more than twice as many disadvantaged 16-18 year-old students studying in colleges as in schools, and in the two years for which there are data this proportion has increased from 71 per cent to 73 per cent suggesting that the gap between schools and colleges is getting even wider. When one provider type is so much less representative, it is a sign of institutional differentiation by social class.

Another symptom of this post-16 polarisation is the 'A Level gap'. A Level programmes have high entry requirements and open the door to 'high status' progression routes. Around a third of A Level students in publicly funded provision are studying in colleges but if we look at the spread of A Level students across institution types, they are unevenly distributed. A Level students represent 80 per cent of the school sixth form final year cohort and 20 per cent of the college final year cohort. This means that school sixth forms are mostly opting out of providing the comprehensive offer needed to meet the needs of all young people.

The comprehensive college

The proliferation of selective sixth forms in some areas has created a de-facto selective system. In contrast, a more comprehensive college can reflect the full profile of the age group.

The ideal of the comprehensive college still exists, despite being under threat as a result of chaotic, incoherent and unplanned patterns of provision. In areas where a comprehensive tertiary approach was implemented, participation, achievement and progression have all increased. Colleges which aim to provide for the educational needs of the full 16-19 age cohort may not always be at the top of performance tables but they are aspirational and successful learning communities. Despite the greater A Level numbers in schools, more disadvantaged students progress to university from colleges than from schools. This includes many students who left school with low GCSE grades and make it to university after three or four years of further education. These are students who wouldn't even get a foot in the door of a selective sixth form and would have been written off as 'no hopers'.

So what are the arguments for selection, whether by prior achievement or educational needs? Why is it so important to separate young people who are going to live and work together?

Proponents of selection at 16 argue that by then we know who the 'academic' students are, and they will do better if they are with other students like them. This kind of deterministic labelling only holds students back, denying them the possibility of growth or change. There's no evidence that equally qualified students do any better in a selective setting.

Another argument is that 'structures don't matter' and all that counts is good teachers and good schools. This fails to recognise the social setting and the messages being sent to students and parents about who and what is and isn't valued. By placing institutional walls between students, for whatever reason, we limit opportunities for achievement and social cohesion and we risk reproducing existing patterns of success and failure.

By providing reasons to turn people away, highly selective providers define aspiration in competitive terms; you have to beat someone else to get your place and where you go becomes more important than what you might achieve. Selection shapes our view of ourselves and each other, limits our horizons and restricts our notions of human potential and progress. We cannot afford the waste and division this represents.

Comprehensive colleges are alive and well and they have a track record of success and the evidence can be seen across the country. But they are surviving in a harsh climate, where the institutional environment, the qualification system and the education market all encourage sorting and ranking of institutions and the creation of hierarchies of students and programmes.

Rethinking curriculum, pedagogy and assessment

16-18 qualification reform in England is moving towards a more binary model based on two main routes: 'academic' leading mainly to HE and 'technical' leading mainly to employment. This doesn't do justice to the diversity of young people's aspirations and journeys and risks locking them into over-specialised programmes with few opportunities to move sideways or broaden their range. This could leave students on both routes ill-equipped for the modern labour market. There is also a lack of any core curriculum entitlement common to all 16-18 year-olds just at the point in their lives where they are becoming full citizens and developing their sense of purpose and agency in society. We need a curriculum for global citizenship and personal growth which helps students develop their social, cultural, political, economic and psychological literacies. Rather than telling so many young people at 16 that they are not 'academic' we could create a single overarching national diploma framework which could keep more learning routes and possibilities open to everyone.

Young people are increasingly highlighting the gaps in their curriculum themselves and asking questions like "where do we learn about the climate emergency? where do we learn about the reality of racism and colonialism, inequality and conflict?". We need to listen and involve students as active and engaged partners, defining their needs and helping to shape their curriculum.

We also need to re-invest in adult education and go beyond an approach based on a minimalist basic skills or retraining offer, important as these are. Adult Education Budgets have been eroded over the last decade and we have lost any national commitment to emancipatory lifelong learning for all. This is treated as a luxury which must be paid for by the student, inevitably limiting the benefits to the better off.

The rapid shift to online learning during this crisis has been impressive and shows the adaptability and flexibility of the FE sector, while also highlighting the risk of deepening existing inequalities, whether in access to devices, prior knowledge and skills, signposting of resources or access to professional support. The use of e-learning has been steadily growing in colleges, with some brilliant innovative practice. But the sudden switch to almost total dependence on remote teaching methods is more than the acceleration of a trend. It prompts some fundamental questions about pedagogy and the planning and organisation of learning.

The cancellation of external exams this summer and their replacement with teacher assessed grades provides us with the opportunity to question our high stakes public exam system which is so dependent on terminal, external assessment and the performance measures and tables which this system feeds. The rediscovery of trust in teacher judgement this year is welcome, and it cannot just be switched off next year. We need to find ways to build on it.

FE as part of a system

We need to move on from the market model and start to think more systemically and find ways to incentivise all post-16 education providers to work together. We need an approach to all 16-18 provision which encourages the kind of co-ordination and collaboration which can ensure that whatever funding there is benefits students and protects the educational offer. Initiatives like the Strategic College Improvement Fund and its successor College Collaboration Fund have helped to support partnership work and sharing of good practice, at least within our sector.

Schools serve neighbourhoods, universities have a broad civic purpose, but colleges are always rooted in a community and often have both a local and regional focus as well as an educational and an economic role.

We need an inclusive and representative 16-18 education system which aims to challenge disadvantage and narrow achievement gaps. We also need a renaissance in adult education, to promote health and personal development and community engagement. Colleges are well placed to fill both these spaces and respond in ways which are driven by the aspirations of the people who live in their localities.

One policy response from the Labour Party has been the idea of a National Education Service (NES). This is an excellent organising principle which still needs to be filled in with concrete examples of how it would broaden opportunity.

I have written elsewhere about the promise of a National Education Service[2]. I think it needs to be grounded in our shared values and to start with a broad debate about what we want from education. An NES could help give purpose and coherence to our ramshackle market of overlapping and competing institutions. This is a proposal which could be a vote winner and has the potential to transform educational opportunity by giving education its 'NHS moment'.

Conclusion

We are living through a time of crisis, fracture and division. If we want to address the many challenges which face us; economic, social, democratic and environmental; inequality, injustice, violence and prejudice, we will need a modern, comprehensive, public education system which is fit for purpose and which can foster a democratic culture in which everyone has a stake. A key element of that system will be a thriving college sector.

We can see the outlines of the college of tomorrow in the best of the colleges of today. They are innovative, creative, ambitious, locally rooted, responsive and inclusive. They will need to be at the heart of any progressive education programme.

References

1   Daley, M, Orr, K. and Petrie, J. (2015) *Further Education and the twelve dancing princesses*, UCL Institute of Education Press.
2   Playfair E. (2018) The Promise of a national education service, *FORUM* 60 (2), 159.

Eddie Playfair *writing in a personal capacity*

What does the future hold for Higher Education?

FOR ALL their brilliance, dedicated staff and millions of graduates who have helped to create modern Britain, our universities and colleges continue to be underwritten by policy and funding systems that perpetuate the inequities of socio-economic class. While the left has long criticised the 11 plus and private schools, it has been slower to critique a selective higher education system and its longstanding Oxbridge[1] obsession. The case for the comprehensive university[2] has been set out by Professor Tim Blackman, Vice-Chancellor of the Open University and formerly Vice Chancellor of Middlesex University, but the history of the UK's universities and especially those in England, tell a different story.

While the number of universities steadily increased in Europe and in Scotland where four universities had been founded by 1582[3], Oxford (founded circa 1167) and Cambridge (circa 1209) maintained a monopoly in England marked by its conservatism and a requirement that all those who graduated had to be Anglicans. This lasted until 1826 when a secular college was funded in London which subsequently became University College with degrees validated by the University of London, itself founded as a validating body by Royal Charter. Durham was founded as a church university in 1832. Thereafter progress was glacial although the potential prestige of a university began to dawn on civic leaders in the 19th century's expanding industrial cities such as Liverpool, Manchester and Birmingham. By the beginning of the 20th century, England lagged behind some of its own imperial dominions, the US, Spain, France and Germany in terms of the number of universities per head of the population – a situation which continued until after 1945.

The influence of Oxbridge has extended far beyond their college walls. From 1603 both Universities were parliamentary constituencies in their own right, each entitled to elect two Members of Parliament - an arrangement that remarkably lasted until 1950. With the exception of Gladstone, Oxford's MPs were Tories (usually elected unopposed). Cambridge's representatives included a few Whigs but the majority were drawn from Conservative ranks. Their electorates were their male graduates. Women students were only included after 1918 when the UK's female franchise was extended – 'students' being the operative word. Oxford only amended its regulations to allow its women students to graduate in 1920. Cambridge clung onto its discriminatory practices until 1948[4].

An Oxbridge degree provided a passport into the higher echelons of the civil service and the political elite – and still does. A classics degree was regarded as an appropriate qualification for colonial postings in the British Empire. After the 2019 general election, 44 of the UK's 55 Prime Ministers had graduated from either Oxford or Cambridge. More than half had studied at one of 3 private schools - Eton College (20), Harrow School (7) and Westminster School (6). [5]

While Oxbridge was guarding its male ivory towers, the 19th century saw the working class beginning to access advanced education through a multitude of Mechanics Institutes, evening classes and an incipient trade union movement. Bradford had a Female Education Institute, Halifax a Working Men's College. In Yorkshire there was a Union of Mechanics Institutes while the origins of the University of Central Lancashire (UCLan) in Preston can be traced to the prosaically named 'Institution for The Diffusion of Useful Knowledge' in 1828.

From 1836 some government grants were awarded for Schools of Art and Design. After 1889 local authorities had the power to levy rates and divert 'whiskey money' to local technical education. Public subscription funded institutions like the Borough Polytechnic Institute[6] in Southwark which opened its doors in 1892 'to promote the industrial skill, general knowledge, health and well-being of men and women.' Paisley Technical College[7] established in 1897 was one of many, while Cardiff School of Art[8] (Science was added later) began teaching in the city's Old Free Library in 1865. The expansion of elementary education triggered a new wave of teacher training colleges, many under a religious banner, although the first non-denominational college was created in 1885 at Edge Hill[9].

Alongside their own monumental struggles for recognition and improved working and social conditions, trade unions funded new education opportunities often through evening classes and public lectures. In 1883, 1000 miners were reported to have lost wages to attend workers' lectures in Newcastle on science, history and the political economy'[10]. From 1903 the Workers Education Association, an alliance of trade unions, the co-operative movement and university extension authorities, promoted 'the higher education of working men' (sic). Too often side-lined by the early and predominantly male trade unions, women organised in their own unions and from 1884 the Women's Co-operative Guild provided further education that went well beyond co-operative principles.

Ruskin Hall (College) was set up in Oxford to provide a free university standard education via evening classes, correspondence courses and residential study. Its location was a deliberate decision to challenge the bourgeoise education offered by Oxford University to the upper class. After the original American benefactors withdrew, Ruskin was funded by trade union scholarships – only extended to women in 1919. The teaching of sociology, evolution and Marxian economics proved controversial. By 1909 there was a student strike, the result in part of disagreements between those of the College's administrators who favoured the economics of gradualism and others committed to a more radical working-class education. Ruskin continued but the Plebs League and the Central Labour College were offshoots of the dispute. Both were committed to a radical vision of education which went beyond learning a trade. Largely funded by the South Wales Miners Federation and what became the National Union of Railwaymen, they lasted until after the 1926 General Strike,

This rich, diverse and dynamic history lived on in evening classes, part-time study, in the involvement of mature students and wider access to advanced qualifications. Nonetheless, by the 1950s the UK still had only 25 universities which were reluctant to expand. The Treasury-funded Universities Grants Committee recognised that additional university places were required to assuage demand from the post-war baby boom and the 1944 Education Act which had made secondary education free[11]. From 1961-65 eight new universities were created on green field sites[12]. They were awarded university title straight away and funded for teaching and research. All were based on the Oxbridge assumption that students would leave home, study full-time and be considered for admission if they had at least two A-levels.

The 1963 Robbins Report pointed out there were also Colleges of Advanced Technology (CATs), Technical and Regional Colleges, Colleges of Commerce, Schools of Art and others all offering advanced higher education qualifications and a strong tradition of successful part-time study including by those with lower pre-entry qualifications. Some of the CATs became universities including Loughborough, Salford and Aston. The Report was adopted by the incoming Labour Government of Harold Wilson but as with the 1944 Education Act delivered by Clement Attlee's Government, there was a sting in the tail which preserved the dominance and elitism of the Oxbridge model.

The Attlee administration had embraced the selection of children at 11 into what was initially envisaged as a tripartite system of grammar, technical and secondary modern schools. The technical schools were not widely adopted. The grammars were much better funded and restricted in student numbers - and the myth of social mobility via the grammar school of the 1950s and 60s was borne. In 1967 Anthony Crosland, Labour's Education Secretary, responded to Robbins, not by establishing new universities, but by creating 30 polytechnics based on local authority bids to expand or combine existing colleges and institutions which were delivering advanced qualifications[13].

Unlike the universities which were autonomous, the new polytechnics were placed under the control of the local authorities. They rapidly demonstrated the extent of the latent demand and waste of talent that was the hallmark of a protectionist university system. Expanding numbers beyond all expectations, they developed new, innovative full and part-time courses and continued the long tradition of flexible modes of study with the majority of their students travelling from work or home to study. Rather than challenging the higher education hierarchy, Labour had created a new one.

The polytechnics were poorly funded in comparison to the universities. Unlike the new universities of the early 1960s, the polys were not granted degree-awarding powers. In spite of the fact that many had been offering advanced qualifications for years, they had to go cap in hand to have their degrees validated by the Council for National Academic Awards[14]. This arrangement did nothing to disturb a value system that put the polys and their graduates lower down the food chain in terms of prestige and the unit of resource per student.

Ironically, it was the Thatcher government's 1988 Education Act which cut the ties between local authorities and their polytechnics and colleges. Vice-Chancellors who were polytechnic Principals at the time, considered this was less to do with any grand educational vision and more to do with the visceral dislike of local authorities of Sir Keith Joseph, Thatcher's Education Secretary and an early convert to the market and monetarism. The Polytechnics and Colleges Funding Council and a Universities Funding Council were created. The polytechnics had been granted the same autonomous status as universities but still lacked their own degree-awarding powers. Ignoring their record in contract research and postgraduate courses, they were still not allocated any funding for research.

John Major, Thatcher's successor as Prime Minister, was persuaded of the merits of finally removing Crosland's binary divide – especially since the cost of doing so was marginal. The 1992 FE and HE Act was passed with cross-party support, established a single Higher Education Funding Council (HEFCE) and allowed polytechnics and other higher education institutions to apply for university title and taught and research degree-awarding powers on the same terms as the established universities. The change proved hugely popular with students who understood that notwithstanding their achievements, the polytechnics did not enjoy the same status as a university.

This has not prevented politicians from all parties[15], media pundits and political staffers[16] from expressing regret at the demise of the polytechnics, ignoring the fact that as universities, they continue to provide professionally and technically focused courses. Claims that too many people are studying for degrees, that some are not 'proper' universities and teach 'mickey mouse' degrees (an inaccurate allusion to courses related to the UK's world-leading creative industries, worth more to the UK Exchequer than pharmaceuticals) are regularly parroted in the media[17].

Thirty years on, the Conservative Government responded to the coronavirus pandemic by perpetuating the protectionism that has been the hallmark of an elite university system. Reports suggested that Ministers were considering sector 'restructuring' and that some universities might lose access to research funding. The Research Sustainability Taskforce established by Ministers in May 2020 did not include one modern university Vice-Chancellor[18]. Overriding objections from their Scottish, Welsh and Northern Ireland counterparts, Ministers initially responded to the predicted collapse in income from international students arising from the COVID pandemic by limiting the number of loans available for first-year students from England who wished to study elsewhere in the UK. The rationale for a measure which undermined student choice was crystal clear. According to Ministers the objective was to boost numbers in 'high-performing' English universities at the expense of courses they consider to be 'low quality'[19] – a direct interference in the market which they had created to favour some universities at the expense of others.

For all the talk about a mass higher education system, 1992 was not the moment when the barriers of privilege came tumbling down. Vice-Chancellors of universities which had historically received the most research funding and had medical schools met at the Hotel Russell in London to establish the Russell Group to lobby for their own interests. Not to be outdone, a group of smaller self-styled 'research intensive' universities formed the equally unimaginatively named '1994 Group.' This survived until 2012 when four of the group jumped ship having covertly applied to the Russell Group. Belatedly the Coalition of Modern Universities was set-up. Unsurprisingly it did not have the same influence as the others in the corridors of power or in Universities

UK, the trade association which is meant to lobby for the whole sector.

In spite of a manifesto commitment that 50% of those aged 18-30 should progress to university, any hope that the 1997 New Labour Government might upset the hierarchical apple cart were soon dashed. Other OECD countries were already achieving a 50% participation rate but it was New Labour's means of delivery that proved controversial. As with other New Labour policies, the 2003 *The Future of Higher Education White Paper*[20] laid the foundation for the further marketisation of higher education and the trebling of tuition fees by the Conservative and Liberal-Democrat Coalition government in 2012.

Labour's White Paper referred to a boost in research funding and a new system of research assessment. As Margaret Hodge, then Labour Minister for Life-long Learning and Higher Education, advised the Education Select Committee the government wanted 'to concentrate funding on the world class institutions and secondly on those that demonstrate that they are on the upwards escalator "[21]. In other words, the 25 universities which already received 75% of taxpayer funded research money would receive even more. Students were referred to as 'consumers' who needed more information to make their university choices. There was a reference to an assessment of teaching excellence – revived in the 2017 Conservative manifesto and transformed by Conservative Ministers into a bureaucratic Teaching Excellence Framework (TEF) with the potential for TEF outcomes to be linked to institutional tuition fees.

Unlike research, New Labour did not boost higher education teaching funding by an increase in direct grant. Instead the 2004 HE Act permitted universities to charge new full-time students tuition fees of up to £3000pa from 2006. Fees were additional to HEFCE funding (unlike the Tories £9250 which replaced the latter) and the system was referred to a Graduate Contribution Scheme with payback based on actual graduate earnings over and above £15,000 pa. The pill was sugared by the reintroduction of maintenance grants, further extended when Gordon Brown became Prime Minister. After an initial fall, full-time student numbers rose but as modern universities and the OU pointed out, New Labour had left part-time students high and dry with no access to fee loans. Universities which had kept the faith in terms of flexible modes of study were left having to subsidise the costs of part-time tuition.

New Labour's No 10 Strategy Unit considered whether universities should be allowed to fail and there was an expectation at least by some, that universities might charge different fees and, by their own volition, boost the market that the White Paper implied. It was an argument that the Treasury and the Coalition Government returned to in 2010 and one that echoes through the 'best vs worst' university discourse, aided and abetted by the Robbins 'principle' that 'courses of higher education should be available for all those who are qualified by ability and attainment to pursue them and who wish to do so'. Although oft cited this is not the nirvana that it might appear. In spite of the OU admitting its first students in 1971 and continuing to provide access to many higher education courses regardless of pre-entry qualifications, what constitutes 'qualified by attainment' remains hotly contested, undermining the long tradition of working-class education where potential and prior life experience were highly valued.

The universities which are the most successful in admitting students from a wide range of backgrounds, ethnicities and ages are routinely branded as failures for providing opportunities for some students with lower entry qualifications. League tables, big business after 1992 for the commercial organisations which publish them, routinely take account of pre-entry qualifications and research funding. Former Labour Education Secretary, Alan Johnson, signed off the introduction of A* A-level grades to further delineate the allegedly most qualified students - and it was the 2005 New Labour Government which junked the Tomlinson report in favour of the retention of A-levels as 'the gold standard". The Universities and College Admissions Service (UCAS) now categorises universities according to their alleged selectivity regardless of the potential of students or the actual UCAS points of the students recruited by universities which are alleged to be 'high performers'.

But it was Michael Gove, Conservative Education Secretary from 2010, who went the extra mile to reinforce the hierarchy of an elite university system and the Russell Group as a brand. School performance indicators were amended to incentivise progression to the '30 most selective universities'. The Russell Group was funded to advise Ofqual on the content of A-levels which largely became exam-only disregarding the fact that many universities teach and assess students by modules rather than simply rely on end-of-year exams. Ignoring the views of employers, schools and the needs of the creative industries, Gove introduced the spurious EBacc 'qualification' – which is not a qualification but a set of subjects which the Russell Group identified as 'facilitating' admission to their universities.

New Labour at least referred to widening participation and funded the well-regarded 'Aim Higher' programme. After 2010 Coalition and Conservative Ministers, aided and abetted by the Sutton Trust, the media and universities at the top of the 'value' tree, promoted a new myth about social mobility – "fair access of younger students from disadvantaged backgrounds" to a limited number of universities – a theme enthusiastically pursued by Alan Milburn, former Labour Minister who was appointed Social Mobility Tsar. This biased and limiting version of social mobility ignores the third of students who progress to university when they are over 21, assumes that all potential students either want or are in a position to make a choice about living away from home and ignores the fact that 'favoured' universities may not offer courses that these students want to pursue.

This myth (in reality the social stratification to which Blackman refers) plays into the recruitment practices of employers, including 'top' companies which use a 'milk-round' restricted to a small group of universities – institutions which admit far fewer students from state and non-selective schools, almost no mature students and in many cases notoriously low numbers of Black students. These elitist practices are given further credibility when the same universities are routinely referred to as the 'best' universities. Having benefitted from years of preferential funding, they can trade on historic reputations reinforced by a media and political narrative which is endorsed by politicians and commentators who are too often themselves alumni of the same universities.

From 2010, Coalition and Conservative governments applied with gusto free market principles to the higher education market alluded to in Labour's 2003 White Paper. Full-time tuition fees trebled to £9250pa for new students, replacing over 80% of teaching grant including an allowance for postgraduate taught courses. Higher fees and the deregulation of student numbers led to the rapid expansion of Russell Group universities at the expense of others. Although given access to fee loans, potential part-time students balked at the new ticket price and their numbers fell like a stone. Maintenance grants were scrapped with the inevitable result that students from the poorest households accrue the highest levels of debt. The abolition of NHS bursaries for nursing and other health professional students and their replacement by the higher education fee and loan system led to a downturn in applications from mature students.

The value of a degree began to be assessed in terms of graduate salary outcomes disregarding regional wage variations, gender and BAME pay gaps, the lower initial salaries of graduates who enter the creative industries and the fact that family background remains the major determinant of early graduate career progression. Meanwhile the allocation of research funds became even more selective.

All of this was progressed under the banner of widening opportunities but there was little disguising the fact that an HE market was the end game. The Treasury and Ministers expected universities which they considered to be of less value to charge lower fees. When the majority of modern universities indicated that they would charge the maximum, some were invited by Vince Cable, the then Secretary of State, to justify the decision of their Boards of Governors. Vice-Chancellors pointed out that a lower fee would reduce the unit of resource for students from the most disadvantaged. When one Vice-Chancellor had the temerity to suggest that if the government was serious about social mobility, Ministers should require Oxbridge to lower their fees until they recruited the same inclusive student cohort as his university, the meeting soon ended. The Conservative Government's 2017 Higher Education and Research Act (HERA) made clear that HE was a market at least when it came to student recruitment and established the Office of Students (OfS), a regulator on the lines of Ofcom and Ofwat.

For all the focus and justified angst about fees, the concentration of research funding in a small number of UK universities has been one of the most significant factors in limiting opportunities for students and staff. Research is a major driver of inequity in the student resource and in access to facilities underwritten by capital investment in research infrastructure. The Research Excellence Framework by which Quality Related (QR) funding is allocated to institutions for 5 years based on historic peer review, is itself worth £1.4bn pa. In reality Ministers set the terms on which allocations are made. Astonishingly no QR funding has been allocated to research assessed as of being of national or international significance (2* and 3* research) for years[22]. Unsurprisingly the universities which benefit most from QR are also the most successful in competing for research council grants, further restricting student and staff opportunities. The binary divide may have been abolished in principle but it has been preserved in a protectionist research funding model that benefits disproportionately a small sub-set of universities in a small sub-set of geographic areas and acts as a form of stasis, depriving the UK and its wider regions of talent and innovation.

Universities and colleges cannot solve all the consequences of deprivation and inequality but they are key actors in any strategy seeking to deliver social justice. The monetised, non-monetised and inter-generational benefits of higher education are well-known and spill over into positive impacts on society and the economy as well as the individual. But as Labour's 2019 manifesto highlighted, higher education will not be reformed simply by abolishing tuition fees and advanced learner loans and improving student support (although all are crucial to any cradle to grave National Education Service).

In its commitment to end the free market, 'rethink the assessment of research and teaching quality and develop a new funding formula that...ensures all public HE institutions have adequate funding for teaching and research, widens access to higher education, reverses the decline in part-time learning (and) ends the casualisation of staff' Labour gave a clear signal that it was ready to break with the funding systems and the politics of higher education elitism which have themselves been causes of disadvantage.

If it is serious about a new vision of the future which values the radical working-class traditions of the past, Labour must abandon the never-ending trope of vocational vs academic education and qualifications. Labour's old Clause 4 had lots of merits but the distinction between 'workers by hand or by brain' was not one of them. The vocational and academic divide should be put to bed as should references to universities as the 'best', 'world-leading', 'high-performing, 'leading' and 'research intensive' – code as everyone knows for the Russell Group and a hierarchical and class-based policy and funding framework that damages the cause of social justice. These descriptors undermine the value of other universities (the majority). Just as important they devalue the achievements of the majority of students, graduates and staff and ignore the fact that all universities in the UK are subject to a quality assurance system.

Reframing higher education is a monumental challenge and one that will undoubtedly be fiercely resisted by those who have benefitted most. A Labour Government can emulate its predecessors and promote access to higher education but continue to reward and promote a narrow view of excellence. It can perpetuate private schools, the 11 plus and a university admissions system largely based on selection at 18. It can pitch investment in one part of the education sector against investment in another (early years vs higher education is a favourite). It can argue that further education colleges are more important than universities – or it can recognise that, as the coronavirus pandemic has shown, there is no shortage of funds if there is the political will.

Labour's task is to set out a vision and then build a life-long, collaborative and comprehensive National Education Service in which no part and no student is pitched against the other. If the Labour Party and a Labour Government want to transform society, they must rewrite the university script.

Pam Tatlow

Notes

1   The Universities of Oxford and Cambridge
2   https://www.hepi.ac.uk/wp-content/uploads/2017/07/Hepi-The-Comprehensive-University_Occasional-Paper-17-11_07_17.pdf
3   St Andrews (1411), Glasgow (1451), Aberdeen (1495), Edinburgh (1582)
4   Kate Edger was the first woman to graduate from a New Zealand University in 1877 and the first in the British Empire to be awarded a BA degree
5   Labour's 2019 Conference passed a resolution calling for the abolition of private schools but 40 years earlier the Party had published *Private Schools a Labour Party discussion document* 1980
6   The founding institution of London South Bank University
7   The founding institution of the University of the West of Scotland
8   The founding institution of Cardiff Metropolitan University
9   The founding institution of Edge Hill University
10   *The Northumbrians*, North-East England and its People, a New History pg87 Dan Jackson pub 2019
11   The Act also enabled the Secretary of State to raise the school-leaving age from 15 to16 although this was not actioned until 1971
12   Sussex, Keele, East Anglia, York, Lancaster, Essex, Kent, Warwick
13   https://api.parliament.uk/historic-hansard/commons/1967/apr/05/polytechnics
14   http://www.open.ac.uk/cicp/main/validation/awards-and-aftercare/cnaa-pro-forma-verification/about-cnaa
15 https://www.theguardian.com/education/2017/oct/10/former-uk-polytechnics-should-lose-university-status-says-adonis
16   Nicky Timothy, former adviser to Theresa May and grammar school advocate, https://www.telegraph.co.uk/news/2017/08/16/higher-education-has-become-unsustainable-young-people-know/
17   https://www.dailymail.co.uk/news/article-6025073/Too-students-huge-debts-prospect-earning-life-graduates-Britain.html
18   https://www.researchprofessionalnews.com/rr-news-uk-politics-2020-5-research-sustainability-taskforce-details-confirmed/
19   https://www.theguardian.com/education/2020/jun/01/plan-to-cap-numbers-at-uk-universities-to-go-ahead
20   http://www.educationengland.org.uk/documents/pdfs/2003-white-paper-higher-ed.pdf
21   https://publications.parliament.uk/pa/cm200203/cmselect/cmeduski/425/425.pdf
22   Details of research funding methodologies and allocations are published by UKRI https://re.ukri.org/documents/2019/how-we-fund-heis-pdf/
23   Ian Duckett, Pam Tatlow and James Whiting, Towards a Comprehensive 14-19 Curriculum: a Socialist Perspective, *Education for Tomorrow* Issue 3, September, 2019 and Ian Duckett, Pam Tatlow and James Whiting, 'Towards a new 14¬19 curriculum', *Education Politics*, 139, September, 2019

Contributors

Ian Duckett was a teacher and head of an alternative education provision in London. He is currently a consultant and school improvement partner in Norwich, a member of National Executive Committee of Socialist Educational Association and an executive committee member of Norfolk NEU.

Naomi Fearon was the Deputy General Secretary of the SEA and is currently chair of the Greater Manchester branch. She is a specialist in SEND provision and works in an independent special school.

Melanie Griffiths was a maths and SEN teacher. Now she is a supply teacher, a member of the NEU's supply teacher organising forum and on Kirklees NEU EC. She is currently Chair of the SEA.

Philipa Harvey was national president of the NUT and is currently a member of the union's national executive. She is a primary teacher.

Daniel Kebede is a teacher and the senior vice president elect of the NEU.

Karen Parkin is Wigan district secretary in the National Education Union and a member of the union's national executive.

Eddie Playfair is a Senior Policy Manager at the Association of Colleges (AoC), he taught in Secondary and Further Education for 35 years and was a college principal from 2002 to 2018.

Jane Rea worked as an early years teacher, OFSTED inspector and LA adviser before taking up ownership and management of the Curious Goose Nursery in Devon.

Tony Rea had a successful career as a secondary school teacher before moving into higher education; he is now retired and is a local councillor in Ivybridge, Devon.

Louise Regan was national president of the NUT/NEU. She is currently national officer for membership and equality. She is also joint editor of the SEA bulletin *Education Politics*. She is a primary teacher.

Karen Parkin is member of the executive of the NEU

Chris Smith teaches politics and history in Norwich where he is also a Labour Party and Norfolk NEU EC member.

Pam Tatlow has taught in comprehensive schools and colleges, worked for a number of trade unions and was Chief Executive of MillionPlus, the Association for Modern Universities, from 2004-2018.

Kiri Tunks was national president of the NEU. She is a secondary teacher.

James Whiting was a secondary drama teacher in London and a senior leader in two schools, specialising in the curriculum for the 14 to 19 phase, also working for Hounslow LA. He is General Secretary of the SEA.

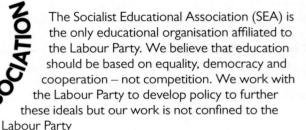

What is the Socialist Educational Association?

The Socialist Educational Association (SEA) is the only educational organisation affiliated to the Labour Party. We believe that education should be based on equality, democracy and cooperation – not competition. We work with the Labour Party to develop policy to further these ideals but our work is not confined to the Labour Party

Labour now promises to:
● End the academies programme, abolish Ofsted and high stakes testing
● Bring all schools and central services back to democratic properly funded local authorities.
● End deregulation, privatisation and under-funding of our public services.

How does the SEA organise?
● We discuss alternatives to the Tory narrow test-driven curriculum that is currently stifling our schools and colleges.
● We show how another system is possible. We develop alternative policies for teaching, learning and assessment.
● We campaign with unions, parents and other groups to resist the damage that the Tories cause.
● We oppose privatisation and casualisation of staff in school, college or university

How do I find out more?
Go to www.socialisteducationalassociation.org to:-
● Find out about news and events
● Read editions of our journal *Education Politics*

How do I join?
Membership is open to all with an interest in Lifelong Learning.
Fill in the membership form at the back of this pamphlet or join via our website.
The SEA has active branches across England, as well as SEA Cymru, our Welsh branch, which organise their own programme of events.

Melanie Griffiths

SOCIALIST EDUCATIONAL ASSOCIATION - MEMBERSHIP FORM

Affiliated to the Labour Party   *www.socialisteducation.org.uk*

I WANT TO JOIN / REJOIN THE SEA AND PAY THE FOLLOWING SUBSCRIPTION —

Single: Waged £25 ☐ or Unwaged £12 ☐   **Couple**: Waged £35 ☐ or Unwaged £18 ☐

DECLARATION: (please tick one):   I am already a member of the Labour Party ☐

Or I am <u>not</u> a member of another political party (and therefore eligible to join the SEA) ☐

CONTACT DETAILS (BLOCK CAPITALS)

First name 1 _____   Last name 1 _____

First name 2 _____   Last name 2 _____

Address _____

Town/City/County _____

Postcode _____   Phone _____

Email _____

Please complete and sign this form and send it to:
SEA Membership Secretary c/o 44 Bruce Road, London E3 3HL

My Local (Education) Authority is: _____

My Parliamentary Constituency is: _____

My trade union is: _____

PAYMENT METHOD (please choose one)

Paying by bank <u>standing order</u> saves time and money.

Ⓐ I attach a cheque made payable to "SEA" for £ _____

Ⓑ I authorise my bank to make regular standing order payments to the SEA as below:

Name of bank/building society _____

Postal address of bank/building society _____

Name(s) of account holder(s) _____

SORT-CODE _____   ACCOUNT NUMBER _____

INSTRUCTION TO BANK

Starting on (date) _____ / _____/201____
please pay SEA the sum of £ _____ and continue
paying the same amount each year on the _____ (day) of
_____ (month). *[For instance, "1st (day) of January (month)"]*
This instruction replaces all earlier ones.

Signed _____   ____/_____/201__

PLEASE PRINT NAME HERE

PAYEE DETAILS

Payee: Socialist Educational Association

c/o Unity Trust Bank PLC, Nine Brindleyplace, Birmingham B1 2HB

Sort Code: 60 83 01
Account No: 50726172

Please quote the reference below (leave blank for SEA admin to supply)

Version: November 2016